MIKE & ME

MIKE & ME

MIKE MURPHY

TOWN HOUSE
DUBLIN

Published in 1996 by
Town House and Country House
Trinity House
Ranelagh, Dublin 6
Ireland

British Library Cataloguing in Publication Data. A catalogue record for this book is available from the British Library.

ISBN 1–86059–029–2

Cover photograph by Dominic Lee, Priory Studios, Dublin.

Typesetting by Red Barn Publishing, Skeagh, Skibbereen
Printed in Ireland by ColourBooks Ltd., Dublin

I dedicate this book to that small circle of people I both love and like. They know who they are and I hope they return the sentiments.

Contents

Let's Hear it for the Patriot

'Here, try this,' said Denis Meehan, handing me a sheet of paper. Denis, silver haired, florid and witty, was the Head of Announcers at Radio Éireann. I, on the other hand, at 23 years of age, had a few problems. For a start, I was getting married in a couple of months and everyone (my wife to be, my mother, my prospective mother-in-law, my entire family circle, in fact) believed I should get myself a Good, Steady, Pensionable Job!

My second problem arose as a direct result of the first. I had no idea what sort of a job I wanted or what sort of job I was suited to. At this stage, having failed with some distinction at school, and having had a remarkably undistinguished early business career, I was 'doing a bit of acting', as well as producing one or two sponsored programmes.

I had seen an ad in the paper for 'announcers' at our national radio station, and felt that this might offer at least some opportunity for a continuation of the variety I enjoyed in my life. So, I sent in the requisite form with a glowing account of my scholastic achievements (none of them true, of course) and a short thesis on my thoughts about, and aspirations in, broadcasting.

Some time later, I was called for interview. The conversational part of the session seemed to go quite well, but then I was handed a typed news bulletin, pointed at the studio and asked to read same. Here my acting experience stood me in good stead. I was able to inject what I felt was the right amount of emotion into the more boring bits of the news, while adopting a more languid, low-key approach to the interesting parts. All in all, I seemed to have 'acted' the news quite well.

But then came a *very bad moment*. The next page was in Irish! Undaunted, however, I decided to attack. The words meant little or nothing to me, despite the best efforts of my teachers at Terenure College, but I did my damnedest to sound like the man who did the voice-over on the *Gael Linn* newsreel in the cinemas.

It didn't work. I knew as I left that the 'role' would not be mine. Some weeks later, I received a letter thanking me for my interest, and wishing me well in my career – any other career! But all was not lost. Within a few days Denis Meehan phoned. He thanked me for attending, sympathised with my undoubted disappointment, and suggested that there just might be a glimmer of hope. He told me that I was quite good in English, but that my command of the native tongue left a great deal to be desired. He suggested that I should take some lessons in Irish and then re-apply, and, assuming my newly conquered *blas* and understanding were acceptable, I could be included on the announcers' course.

Still imbued with a spirit of adult responsibility, I betook myself to the home of Pádraig Ó Mealoid, who was one of the foremost newsreaders *as Gaeilge*. Pádraig was kindly, tolerant – and mildly amused.

Within a few weeks, I was almost adequately equipped to handle, if not the meaning, then certainly the sounds of the language. I phoned Denis to tell him that I believed I was now sufficiently competent to take my place among the chosen. He suggested I come into the station one evening and run through a short test. I was happy to agree.

So here I was, accepting, with some trepidation it must be admitted, the sheet of paper containing the Irish script. I went into the studio and set about the task. When I emerged, Denis came up to me with a wry smile.

'That wasn't bad at all. But did you know what it meant?'

'Oh God, yes,' I said 'It was the introduction to a football commentary.'

'No,' he mused, 'It was part of an oration over Wolfe Tone's grave.' Silence. 'But,' he went on, 'you sounded as though you very nearly understood it.'

Years later, Brigid Kilfeather, who was Denis's assistant at the time, and who was at no stage, then or later, overly impressed with the huge talent I had placed at their disposal, confirmed my suspicions when she told me that I had got in 'over her dead body'.

A Dark Beginning

Mine was not a particularly happy childhood. For over thirty years my parents had lived, for the most part, a 'silent' marriage. There were occasions when we, their five offspring, lived an almost normal family life, but these occasions were few and short-lived.

There was a perennial 'atmosphere'. Whenever the hall door opened as my father returned from work, the temperature in the living room dropped. Those who could, made their excuses and left. If it was a mealtime, mother and children would endeavour to carry on some semblance of a normal conversation, but all was dominated by my father's overpowering silence. His face set in a frigid, humourless mask, he would requisition salt, pepper and so on in a clipped, toneless voice. My mother would relentlessly ask him if he was alright, if his food was warm enough, if he would like more bread and so on, in a bright, chatty voice. I now believe she did this in order to highlight, for the benefit of her children, his bad-tempered demeanour. It was imperative for my mother that she be utterly assured of the unquestioning love and loyalty of all her children, and that, conversely, her husband be alienated from any such affection – as, she believed, his behaviour warranted.

Recently, I said to my youngest brother, John, that if there is such a thing as the 'hereafter', I had no wish to meet either my mother or father again. On reflection, this was desperately unkind. No one, not even family, has the right to judge another person's life. And these two ill-matched individuals lived together for 34 years exactly – right up to the day when my mother was tragically killed on her thirty-fourth wedding anniversary.

They were married on 8 January 1941. While death, pestilence and savagery ravaged the so-called civilised world, the nation of Ireland stood physically and metaphorically to one side. The wedding photograph reveals a decidedly good-looking young couple on, supposedly, the happiest day of their lives. The wedding group is small, no more than eight people, none of whom I recognise. My father is the dominant figure – tall, film-star handsome, a mop of black wavy hair, well-defined features and a lop-sided grin. He is wearing a dark double-breasted suit and looks quite at ease. My mother, wearing a fur coat and small dark hat, is linking arms with him and looking, somewhat coquettishly, at the camera. She is dark, petite, and extremely pretty. Neither of their families attended the wedding.

The history of their relationship is unclear, but, from family sources, it is possible to piece together the sequence of events that led to their union, without knowing the details. Both of them were 28 years of age when they married. My mother was marrying 'beneath her', while my father's family appeared to be relieved to be rid of him.

My mother's name was Kitty Kelly and her family origins were in counties Carlow and Limerick. Her father, an authoritarian Victorian, had been a schoolteacher and later became a bookkeeper for a small company in Dublin city. His wife, who had given birth to seven children, died a victim of the Black 'Flu in 1918, when my mother, the second youngest, was four years of age. One of the girls, my Auntie May, who could only have been about twelve or thirteen at the time, became surrogate mother and housekeeper for the family. And Auntie May, who died last year, aged 87, in an advanced state of Alzheimer's disease, spent much of the rest of her life in service to one person or another. She was a gentle, humorous soul who, when her father died many years later, became housekeeper to a cousin of hers, the parish priest at Marino in Dublin. Father Jack, as he was known, was an austere, arrogant man with a brisk, impatient demeanour, who was not kind to Auntie May. She never married and when Father Jack died, leaving her an insulting bequest, she dedicated the rest of her life to visiting and looking after her sisters, nieces and nephews.

Kitty was spoiled by her father. She was a delicate child who aroused his sympathy and concern. According to her surviving sisters, Gretta and Anne, my mother was used to getting her own way. She was pretty, lively and loved attention.

When she was seven or eight, she became seriously ill with 'double pneumonia', as it was known then, and was given the last rites. From that moment she was her father's pet. He was accustomed to dining alone in the dining-room, while his children had their meals downstairs in the kitchen. Now, Kitty was taken from her brothers and sisters and invited to eat her meals upstairs, with her father. They were both waited upon by May. My sister Catherine told me recently that my mother had learned an important lesson – the sicker she was, the more she was loved! The legacy of this period was that she was to suffer constantly from ill health. Certainly in later years she suffered from migraine, nerves, varicose veins and numerous other disabilities and inconveniences. But it was a family joke that there were a number of 'miraculous' recoveries when needs must, or when some attractive social occasion arose.

From the middle 1930s, the family lived in a modest, semi-detached house in Cherryfield Avenue, Ranelagh. I still have some lingering memories of the place. It was quite dark; brocaded curtains kept out much of the light. The drawing room, on the left of the narrow hall, was where my grandfather held court. It was important to knock before entering.

He was a small, portly man, with thinning hair and a grim mouth, who sat in 'his' chair reading, through small wire-rimmed glasses. I remember he had a fob-watch and was extremely dapper. Everyone was on their best behaviour around him. The room had an upright piano with brass candle-holders, and the armchairs had antimacassars, with ashtrays on the arms in the form of little brass bowls resting on leather straps which hung on either side of the arms of the chair. Upstairs, the rooms had bowls and jugs for washing and, if you 'stayed over', Auntie May gave you a stone hot-water bottle wrapped in a towel. Under the bed was a 'potty'. The kitchen was dominated by a big iron range, above which there was a 'pulley' device for drying clothes. There was the mandatory dresser with willow-pattern delph, a large pine table and chairs and, in the corner, an inelegant mangle for rinsing the washing. This was where Auntie May spent much of her teenage years, after being taken from school at around the age of thirteen.

The house was crowded and must have been somewhat tense. The two eldest boys, Jack and Sonny, were studying banking and law respectively. Tommy, who was a bit of a rake, was to die of TB in his early twenties. It was ordained by their father that neither Gretta nor May, the two eldest girls, should 'work' – meaning 'get a job'. Young girls of good breeding just didn't; they waited until a man came along and they married him, or else they became 'old maids' – God forbid.

The two youngest girls, Kitty and Anne, found that, by the time they left St Anne's Convent, social aspirations had succumbed to economic necessity, and they were required to enter the world of commerce. My mother joined the Civil Service. Through all these years she was what was called in those days 'a bit wild'. She was endlessly pursued by boys, craved their attention, coveted those who cast an eye on any of her sisters, and made a habit of staying out till the early hours. I don't believe she was ever sexually involved with any of these young men – she told us later that she was a virgin when she married. How and when she met my father I don't know; it must have been in 1939 or 1940.

My father's background is similar in some respects. His mother was from Midleton in County Cork. His father, as far as I know, was from Dundrum, then a village on the outskirts of Dublin, where my father spent his young life. They owned a sweetshop beside the church in Main Street. His father, a gambler who often went to race meetings in England, died when Da was eight or nine, the youngest of three children, two of them girls. His mother was a formidable woman, large, imposing – a no-nonsense type. She had a habit of adding 'I say' to the end of her sentences and then repeating them, as if you were either deaf or stupid. If she caught you pilfering a few sweets here or there, she'd give you a clatter on the side of the head that would nearly knock you into next week! The shop was the focal point of their lives and, after my grandfather's death, Auntie Hannah, Gran's sister, moved in permanently. A frail, quiet old thing, she was a bit like 'Felix' to Gran's 'Oscar', in *Odd Couple* terms!

To one side of the shop was the parlour, dark and depressing, with hard dining-room chairs, china cabinet, ornaments and, everywhere, cartons and tins of sweets and cigarettes. The stairs, similarly, were lined with boxes piled high and led up to dingy, uncomfortable, unwelcoming bedrooms. The living-room, behind and a few steps down from the shop, was much more comfortable – a kitchen table, a few armchairs and a fire always lighting. And more boxes of sweets. The food was cooked 'out the back'. You left the living-room by the back door and crossed the outdoor passageway into a kind of lean-to, which had a sink, cooker, pots and pans, and so on. This structure had a tin roof and was only enclosed on three sides – there was no door. It seems to have been a cold life for my father. He was forbidden to enter or exit through the shop; he had to use the back door. His mother offered him little in the way of love or kindness. I heard him later refer to her as a 'hard oul' divil'. My mother told me that he never knew much about giving or receiving affection, and had had to grow up 'tough'.

My father's name was Edward and he was known to everyone as 'Ned'. Everyone, that is, except my mother and her family – to them, he was 'Jack'. My mother told me the story. Apparently, in his early twenties, he was told by a lot of people that he bore an extraordinary resemblance to Jack Doyle, the boxer. It obviously appealed to him, so when he met my mother he told her his name was 'Jack' Murphy. By the time she found out the truth, it was too late; she and all her family called him 'Jack' and continued to do so through the years.

As a child, he went to school by train, taking the old Harcourt Street line into the city and walking the short distance to Synge Street. He seems to have had a great deal of regard for 'the Brothers'; he quite admired the way they 'beat the lessons into you'. It must be said, however, that he never demonstrated any violent characteristics towards any of his children. He never struck me. In fact, he never, ever touched me in any way, as far as I can remember, throughout my life with him. But that's another day.

When my father was only fourteen, he ran away to join the army. His mother tracked him down and, since he had lied about his age, had no trouble extricating him from a possible life of military fulfilment. He left school then, at fourteen, and became a motor mechanic. He soon had access to customers' cars and could impress those he wished to impress. And, it seems, he did. He was dashing, courteous, amusing and was a good soccer player. He played for Bohemians, and told me once about marking the great Len Shackleton who, it appears, gave him a bit of a run-around.

By the time he met my mother, he had become a foreman in Linders' garage in Smithfield. The Linders family loved him and remained his friends for the rest of his life.

He was either too self-conscious, or was made to feel too unwelcome, to call to the door of the house in Cherryfield Avenue when taking my mother out on a date. According to Gretta, 'he would wait in the car at the end of the road for her'. Kitty's father disapproved. The younger man was a mere motor mechanic and, besides, he wouldn't 'look after' the delicate girl sufficiently well.

The impression garnered by my brothers and sisters is that, although he was attracted to my mother and probably flattered by her attentions, he had no intention of settling down. But my mother was encountering problems at home. Her father forbade her to see the young mechanic any more. My mother rebelled. She responded by announcing that she was 'moving out', and that evening she did so. None of her sisters know where she went, except that it was to 'digs' on the south side of the city. Certainly, she didn't move in with her 'paramour'. Instead, she informed him that she had left home to spend the rest of her life with him. He seems to have been a little less than overjoyed at the news but, within a few days, made the expected response and asked her to marry him. Towards the end of his life, he described my mother at this time, to my sister Catherine, as a 'child-woman – spoiled, difficult and delicate'.

There are conflicting accounts of the wedding. According to my mother, she invited her father, brothers and sisters, but they refused to attend. Gretta and Anne maintain that she invited her father only, and not them. They also suggest that my mother arrived at the door a couple of days before the wedding and was given a sum of money by her father. One way or another, the wedding, a very low-key affair, took place in Haddington Road Church. And my mother said later that she caught a glimpse of Gretta and May watching from behind a pillar.

My father's family were anything but euphoric, either. His mother had taken an instant dislike to Kitty – which was heartily reciprocated, by the way – regarding her as altogether 'too full of herself', and her family as 'jumped-up snobs'. But his mother seems to have been glad enough to get rid of Ned and, immediately after the wedding, burned all his remaining possessions, including photographs of him as a child, boy and young man. I never saw a photograph of my father taken before he was married. There was no reception, just a few drinks afterwards, then the newly-weds went straight to their new home, the first of what was to be their – and our – fourteen homes, a flat in 136 Rathgar Road. According to family legend, my father dropped my mother off at the flat, told her there was some food in the cupboard, said goodbye and went back to work. My mother sat down at the kitchen table and burst into tears.

11

But the story of the 'big day' didn't end there. Many years later, my mother told one of my sisters that, on their wedding night, my father sat on the edge of the bed, put his head in his hands and cried.

Senseless in Suburbia

Nine months and twelve days later, on 20 October 1941, Kitty and Ned Murphy were pleased to announce the arrival of the first fruit of their relationship – me – Michael James.

The happy occasion seems to have brought about a slight diminishing of the family tensions. My grandfather looked at me and, according to my mother, he prophesied that 'Michael will always look after his mother'. As far as I'm aware, there was no palpable reaction from my father's side. Certainly, my grandmother didn't send out a photographer to record the momentous arrival!

My memories of the following years are, naturally, hazy. In what photographs there were of me as a baby, I appear pretty nondescript, fairly placid, big head and bald. As I grew older, I became white-blonde, curly-haired and a bit drippy. My brother Declan was born two years later. He was dark, tubby and lovable. We were, and are, very close as brothers and friends.

My memories of our time in Rathgar Road are impressionistic. I remember falling down the steep, stone steps outside the hall door and hurting myself. There was Miss McMahon, an old lady who lived upstairs and whom my mother 'adopted'. 'Miss Mac' was to visit us regularly for years after, until her death.

I remember getting sick with dizziness, swinging from a rope tied to the letterbox across the road, an experience which has, ever after, prevented me from going on any of those fairground rides – like 'chair-o-planes' – which go round and round. (I don't mind roller-coasters, love them in fact, but they go up and down!) There was the time I let the handbrake off my father's car while he was having his dinner (it would be 'lunch' nowadays), and the car reversed slowly out into, and down, Rathgar Road. A passer-by saw my plight, or heard my yelps of fear, and clambered aboard to save the day.

Another day of great drama was when my baby sister Pat, who at that time was crawling around the floor, reached up and pulled a kettle of boiling water down on top of herself. She was seriously scalded. I can recall the long wait for the doctor, my mother and father bringing her to hospital, and the tension as we waited for Pat to be taken off the danger list. I remember how, at the time, my mother had the presence of mind to douse Pat in flour – apparently this was supposed to help minimise the damage done by the boiling water.

I remember, too, playing football with my father against the garage door with another boy, Arthur Ryan (now 'Mr' Penney's of Ireland), and breaking my heart crying when my mother dropped me off on my first day at Saint Louis National School in Rathmines.

Then there was Barbara Dormer, the 'big girl' from next door, who I think I had a 'crush' on, and who used to mind me and Declan sometimes. She caught her hand in the middle of the see-saw in Palmerston Park. My memory is that her hand was crushed – certainly it was bleeding a lot.

I remember a woman friend of my mother's, Phyllis, bringing Declan and me to Herbert Park for a sunny afternoon stroll. Phyllis sat on a bench, gently rocking Declan in his go-cart, while I went to the water's edge to feed the ducks. Two sailors came along, sat down beside Phyllis, and started to tickle her. Her laughter caught my attention and, to get a better vantage point, I took a couple of steps backwards and fell into the pond. I had to walk, sodden, to my grandfather's house where I was dried out, and Phyllis got 'what-for'.

There was Michael O'Donoghue, whose mother became friends with my mother when we were in our respective prams, and who is still a good friend. When Michael's father, a lovely gentle man from Wexford, died, I recall Michael and myself, on the day of the funeral, playing jackstones on the linoleum of their basement home. I spent that night with Michael and I remember him sobbing for what seemed like hours. We must have been seven or eight. At around that time, Michael's mother took it upon herself to tell me that there was no such thing as Santa Claus, that I was old enough to know the truth. I was devastated. My mother 'freaked out'. I believe it became a major Diplomatic Incident between the two women!

I recall 'poor Mrs Farrell', who lived in Charlemont Street and who used to call regularly (and did so to many subsequent addresses of ours) with her bockety old pram, for any old clothes or left-over food, or whatever. When she drank a cup of tea, she would pour it from the cup and sip it from the saucer.

And there was old Mr Walker, who lived in Hollyfield Buildings, and who wore a stained raincoat with twine around the waist. He had a battered hat, no teeth, and always wore slippers. My mother often used to invite him in for a cup of tea. She was very charitable like that, with a penchant for picking up 'stray' people and being kind to them.

I formed a great attachment to Rathgar Church. My father used to say it was the only church in which he could really pray. As Elizabeth Bowen said about Bowenscourt, when she closed her door in the evening she was 'shutting Ireland out', so it was, and is, with Rathgar Church. It has a dark, vaulted interior, with a dimly-lit passageway around the main body of the church in which are located numerous and mysterious side-altars, with racks of candles and old-fashioned confession boxes. To give a sermon, the priest had to enter a small, almost hidden, door and ascend a winding staircase to emerge, Good

Book in hand, on the pulpit, which projected from the wall high above the faithful. Rathgar Church features large in my past: two family weddings (my sisters Pat and Catherine) and two funerals (my parents). And it was outside Rathgar Church that my mother was killed.

When I was about seven or eight, we moved to Hazelbrook Road in Terenure. The city of Dublin was expanding into the new suburbs, and Hazelbrook Road was an estate in the grounds of an old Big House. It was paradise for Declan and me. Ours was a brand new house and the rest of the estate was still being built, so we had an entire building site as our playground.

There was high drama on the day we moved in. It seems that a man, a black man, had killed himself two doors up from us. The story is, however, a little muddled in my mind, as it is highly unlikely that he hanged himself and then threw himself out of the window of the spare room! But it was a thrilling introduction to our new neighbourhood all the same. There were police, the fire brigade and a smashed front window.

Directly across from our house, which was one of those tidy, post-war, semi-detached homes, was the workmen's hut. This was a block building with a tin roof, which housed tools and other implements and where the men used to sit and have their tea breaks. We used to go over and chat to them on a regular basis. By now, we had formed the nucleus of a gang; there were lots of other children our age nearby, and most of our non-school time was spent climbing up scaffolding and playing 'cowboys and indians' in the half-built structures and the nearby fields. We hero-worshipped some of the men, and gave them nicknames that reflected our interests at the time. One, a big, striking, dark fellow from Cork whose name was Finbar, was accorded the honour of being called 'Hopalong', after our hero, Hopalong Cassidy. His wishy-washy workmate became 'Lucky', Hoppy's sidekick. While a small, bearded man who was, as they say nowadays, orthodontically challenged, became 'Gabby Hayes'.

In the evenings, the hut was occupied by the night-watchman. To us he was known as Tom the 'Gotchy', so-called because of his regular roars whenever he spotted us in forbidden territory. Tom, who always wore a tweed coat and flat cap, had been wounded in the First World War and had a limp, which of course meant that he couldn't catch us when we climbed the scaffolding. Despite the problems we caused him, he seemed to like us. One night he asked us if we would like to see one of his bullet wounds. He rolled up his sleeve and, just below his shoulder, where the main muscle should have been, was a jagged hole with folds of flesh around it. From then on, Tom and his bullet wound became a Major Event. It was possible to persuade other children, not in our gang, to pay us a halfpenny to be brought in to see the bullet wound.

In the field behind the hut was our pride and joy – 'Trigger'. Trigger, a big brown workhorse, was so called because 'Topper', the real Hopalong's horse, was too cissy a name to be given to the steed of our dreams. So, although Roy Rogers was himself too much of a 'drip' to warrant a mention in our neighbourhood unless it was tinged with derision, his horse had a much more acceptable name. We used to throw a sack over Trigger's back, put a rope around his head and ride him slowly around the field. But Trigger was an amiable old thing and was reluctant to do much more than chew, amble and look forlorn. Until, that is, the famous day when the building site was deserted and we took him out to the road for a ride.

We stood Trigger facing down Hazelbrook Road, threw the sack over his back, roped his head and drew lots as to who would be first. I was the lucky one. But I was scared stiff, as indeed, I found out later, was everyone else. We got an orange box and I stood on it, prepared to mount. There was quite a crowd present. Just as I threw my leg over the horse's back, David Daish, who never particularly liked me, nor I him, hit Trigger an almighty whack with a stick that he had been hiding behind his back. Trigger, who was unused to any form of short, sharp action or reaction, let forth an indignant whinny and, with yours very sincerely hanging on with one leg while gripping his mane with both hands, took off at (his) top speed down the length of Hazelbrook Road.

I can remember the sensation of gradually sliding to the left of Trigger's back, and then under his throat. I hung there for as long as I could, but eventually was forced to let go. I have heard since that a horse will never intentionally trample on a person and Trigger, God be good to him, proved the adage that day. As I dropped onto the road, directly under his front hooves, he skidded to a halt. I was shaken, scared and very angry at Mr Daish, who had wisely run in to his mother. From then on, Trigger and I had a very special relationship, which reached a poignant climax some time later when, after the horse had been missing for some days, I asked Hoppy where he was, to be told that he was gone to Keeffe's, the knackers, to be 'turned into glue'.

When we moved to Hazelbrook Road, my sister Patricia was about a year old and Catherine and John were born there, two and four years later respectively. But my mother appeared to be suffering from major bouts of ill health. I recall occasions when an ambulance would arrive at the door in the middle of the night to take her to hospital. By the time John was born, I knew that my mother was extremely unhappy in her marriage. She used to sit myself and Declan down to tell us about her ailments and, intentionally or not, she left us in no doubt that the root cause of much of her illness was her husband, our father. She told us that each time she became pregnant the symptoms and illnesses got worse, but that he didn't seem to understand at all. He, my father, became quieter and more detached. Where, heretofore, he would play soccer with Declan and myself and our friends, now he would nod at us as we played in the road, maybe grunt 'howaya, lads' and enter the house. This is where my abiding memories of the perennial atmosphere in our house began.

We would come in for our meals, spend as little time as possible at the table, and get out again. I remember at this time cautioning myself not to be too friendly to Da in case I would be letting Ma down and appear to be disloyal.

John was born when I was ten, and Ma had a particularly difficult birth. She was in hospital for quite some time afterwards and John, who

I think may have been born prematurely, was a very delicate baby. Years later, we discovered that this was the point when Ma drew the line. She told Da, in no uncertain terms, that the physical side of their marriage was over. Needless to say, there was no question whatsoever of considering artificial means of birth control, and, anyway, there seems to have been more to it than was immediately apparent.

My parents had become very friendly with the family next door, the Lawlors, and particularly with one of the daughters, Ann, a tall, elegant young woman who became a life-long friend to both of them. It was only recently that Ann recalled that time for me. She was especially close to my mother, who had confessed to Ann that she hated the physical side of marriage. She couldn't bear all that close, intimate contact and, anyway, the pregnancies were creating serious health problems for her. She told Ann that she had ended it once and for all. From then on, it was single beds and, later, when we moved to a larger house, separate rooms.

I wonder who my father could have confided in. I suspect no one. He had no intimate friends that I can remember, and certainly he would not have spoken to his family about such matters.

So, here they both were, 38 years of age, with five children to support and educate, and little or no love or intimacy between them. Although their union led to such unhappiness among their children, I can't help but feel desperately sad for both of them. Had they married different partners, they would both probably have been much more content. Had there been some form of counselling available at that time, perhaps they would have been able to reach some form of accommodation. It was unthinkable that they would, or could, separate. It simply wasn't an alternative. My father was, despite his external bravado, a conservative man who would not, under any circumstances, have reneged on his responsibilities. My mother, who was deeply religious, would have been much too proud to admit to failure in her marriage; she was more inclined to simply 'offer it up'. A phrase she used regularly was 'you make your bed and you lie in it'. The fact that this adage was in direct conflict with her own actions did not seem to occur to her.

The Follies of Academia

My schooldays were spent in Terenure College. Well, most of them, anyway. I commenced my scholastic career at the age of seven, and took my leave ten years later, one year short of the Leaving Certificate. Terenure College was, and is, a beautiful place in which to study, if one wished to study – which I didn't really, at the time. It consisted, then, of the old historic house, where hangs the first bell to toll the dawn of Catholic Emancipation, with a very formidable red-brick extension and a then-modern concert hall added on with classrooms overhead. Now, of course, it is more like a campus than a school.

The Carmelite Fathers ran the college, with varying degrees of success. The place was surrounded by fields and had a beautiful lake walk, as well as a small farmyard. There was a spacious yard for playing in, an orchard for robbing, a gymnasium with a tuck shop, two handball alleys and the bicycle shed, where those boys who were disturbingly sophisticated and daring could go for a few pulls of a cigarette during the breaks. It was in the bicycle shed that Harry Perry, a little guy who went on to become one of Ireland's greatest boxers, fought Paddy Hipwell, a big red-headed rugby player and, to our amazement, beat him.

Rugby was the order of the day, every day. When you joined the school you became a member of a 'house'. Mine was St Patrick's and I was made vice-captain of the rugby team almost immediately – a position I held until I left school. If you liked it, rugby became your life. And I loved it. It helped that we had such a good team. Every Wednesday and Saturday we played, during the season, against another school. We quickly found out that we were better and stronger than most of the other school teams. There were some, like Blackrock, Castleknock, Belvedere and Clongowes, who used to make life difficult for us, but for the most part we became accustomed to winning.

And, of course, the first team rugby players at all levels were somehow special. We had to train long and hard but, in the main, the priests were quite understanding about our lack of application in class.

If the world of rugby and sports generally came easily to me, the wonderful world of academia did not! How I managed to stay in the 'A' class for all those years still remains a mystery to me. I know I had a happy knack of seeming to pay attention to what the teacher was saying, from my position about two-thirds of the way down the room. If the teacher caught my eye, I would invariably pause a moment, a goat-like expression on my face, and allow the light of understanding to slowly cross my brow, accompanied by a sagacious nod. This had the desired effect of reassuring most of the teachers that knowledge was being transmitted – if not instantly, then certainly successfully – even to those toward the back of the classroom.

Father Grace, however, didn't fall for my ploy. Father Grace was a rotund, lowsized man from Kilkenny who, I believe, hurled for his county. Certainly, he was very fond of sport. But not soccer. Soccer was a game that I had come to early – through my father – and, along with a few of my friends in Terenure College, we would, as they said at the time, 'have a bit of bootin'' during the school breaks. Father Grace did not approve. He informed us, turning the old adage to his advantage, that 'rugby was a gentlemen's game played by gentlemen, while soccer was a gurriers' game played by gurriers'. And would we mind not playing so close to the cricket crease?

Father Grace it was who christened me 'MM' – Marked Man. He was in charge of the science class and, no matter how often I permitted the glow of knowledge to suffuse my brow, he would fix me with a baleful eye and ask me a question that could as easily have been about trigonometry as science, as far as I was concerned. Father Grace knew I was an unworthy member of his flock.

I do believe, however, that it wasn't just my lack of application at science that caused him to call me 'MM'. Father Grace happened to be watching a rugby match in which I featured. I was fairly quick and we were playing against CBS Monkstown, or one of the lesser lights in rugby terms. I collected the ball from the kick-off and ran through a number of opponents' tackles to find myself in the clear. I had only the fullback to beat, but, instead of veering to one side and beating him for pace on the outside, I thought I'd show off a little and beat his tackle too. So I ran straight at him and tried to sidestep him – unsuccessfully as it turned out. He landed on me and nearly flattened me. We didn't score from that play, although we did win the match.

Father Grace made a brief guest appearance in our pavilion as we changed afterwards to ask me loudly 'what sort of an eejit' was I and that he would be keeping a good eye on me in the future. He did. Weeks later in the science laboratory, two floors up, I was gazing dreamily out at the early fall of snow. Father Grace caught the drift of my gaze and asked me was I enjoying the snow. I told him yes, that I liked snow very much. Father Grace asked me would I like to go out in it. I said that that would be very nice. So Father Grace said, well, out you go then. I thanked him very much, stood up and told him I'd get my coat and wouldn't be too long. He said, no, you won't be getting your coat, and yes, you might be quite a while out there. He told me to go down to where he could see me in the field and he would tell me where I should go.

So I went downstairs and walked out into the field, from where I could see Father Grace leaning out of the window of the classroom. It was snowing fairly heavily by this stage, but Father Grace waved me further out into the field. I headed in the general direction of the walnut tree to get in under it and shelter. But Father Grace indicated no, no, no, more out into the open spaces if you please. I reversed out, looking back at him with a pleading look on my face, but he indicated no, no, that wasn't far enough. So he made me stand out in the middle of the field with the snow coming down on top of me, and every so often he looked out the window to see that I hadn't moved away.

Eventually, I was quite white and very miserable indeed. When I was a sufficient source of amusement for the rest of my class, the Abominable Snowman and all that, Father Grace relented and permitted me to come back to the haven of his classroom. When my mother found out what Father Grace had done she wanted to come up to the school and, at the very least, give him six of the best with the wooden spoon, but I dissuaded her, for fear of being called a sissy.

I have met Father Grace many times since I left school and he has always looked at me with a twinkle in his eye and asked me was I still chancing my arm? To which, of course, I have always responded in the affirmative.

My school reports were always interesting, because I was extremely good at the subjects that I found stimulating and extremely bad at the subjects that bored me. The side of my brain that had to cope with mathematics and science and commerce did not seem to function at all. While the other side, the one that had to absorb history, English and languages, seemed perfectly willing to work. My Intermediate report, when it eventually came, was pretty spectacular. Less than 10% in five subjects and over 70% in five!

But it was Father Hannigan, a quiet, sensitive man who had a comprehensive interest in English literature and in the theatre, who, I believe, set me on the road I was eventually to pursue. At that time, although Terenure College was not altogether successful academically, for the most part it excelled at sport and at drama. Every year the Terenure pupils staged a Shakespeare play. In some instances, the boys did not want to be part of the play, but in many instances it was a welcome diversion from studying. And so people like myself who wanted some distraction were drawn to the school plays.

I started out badly, however. At the age of thirteen, before my voice broke, I was considered for the part of Lady Macbeth. This did not go down at all well with a high-flying wing forward, so I promptly made my feelings known to Father Hannigan. He reconsidered and asked me would I prefer to play the First Murderer. I readily agreed. The idea of portraying a bloodthirsty killer was highly appealing indeed, and when the play went on I enjoyed myself hugely in my small but meaningful role.

The following year I was cast as Edmund, the bastard son in *King Lear*. This was a wonderful meaty role. Early in *King Lear*, Edmund sidles on-stage and launches himself into his big soliloquy: 'Thou Nature art my goddess, to thy laws my services are borne' and, to my great satisfaction, there was actually silence through most of the speech. Gabriel Fallon, who at that time was theatre critic for the *Irish Press*, used to write a piece about the Terenure College play and, in this instance, gave me a terrifically encouraging write-up for my portrayal of Edmund. Cordelia, Lear's youngest daughter, was played, in a long blonde wig, by the fourteen-year-old Donal McCann, who was, of course, destined to become one of Ireland's greatest ever actors. I remember that the wig and dress had a very unsettling effect on the boarders, arousing all sorts of subliminal longings in those young men who were locked into the college for most of the school year. I even recall Donal rejecting invitations to 'come over here and sit on my lap'. Mind you, it has to be said, he made a very fetching Cordelia indeed!

Flushed with success, I was cast the following year as Gratiano in *The Merchant of Venice* – a 'hard case' who dominates the court scene with his superficial interjections. Again, the school audience thought this hugely entertaining and, again, I was able to bask for a day or two in the satisfaction of having achieved a certain notoriety. A major drawback for me in this instance was that I was forced to kiss Paddy Flynn, who was cast, against his will it must be said, as Nerissa. Paddy was, on the rugby field, a fairly chunky fullback, and even the sensuous cut of his long stage dress couldn't mask the lumbering gait of a reluctant cross-dresser. We kissed, it must be said, with mutual distaste.

At some stage during those years, Father Hannigan made a complimentary reference to my voice. I think he was trying to get me to speak louder and he said something about the God-given quality of my speaking voice. I recall, with some embarrassment, him describing it as having a 'velvet quality'. It was the first time anybody had ever mentioned anything about my voice to me – the first time I had even thought about it, in fact. I regret very much, to this day, that Father Hannigan died before I was able to tell him that his off-the-cuff comment had meant a great deal to me. I think of it now in the context of how important it is to encourage young people and not to criticise too much, in order to make them aware of their good points and to open up to them as many opportunities for the future as possible.

In my early teens, my school reports from Terenure College were so abysmal that, despite my mother's protests, my father insisted that I be sent to Synge Street so that the Brothers could straighten me out. I hated the place on sight. After the green fields and open spaces of Terenure College, I found the dark classrooms and bleak walled yard completely oppressive. On the second day, I wore my Terenure cap to school. The boys started hitting me and trying to take it from me, but I held on. I wore it in class too, so the teachers started hitting me. I did it a second day, then a third. By the end of the week, with his brat of a 'college boy' arriving home daily, scratched, bruised and dishevelled, my father gave in. Almost.

The following Monday I was deposited in Colaiste Mhuire on Parnell Square. If Synge Street was bad, this was nightmare stuff! They didn't even *have* a yard – and the classrooms were darker. *And* they all spoke Irish, a language in which I have yet to distinguish myself! By the end of the week I was back in the scholastically questionable – but environmentally delightful – surroundings of Terenure College.

There were many priests and teachers in Terenure College that I remember with the greatest of affection. Father Clarke, Father Hegarty, Father Kinahan, Father McCouaig, Father Ryan, Father Devane, Mr Griffin, Mr O'Connell, Mr Fitzsimons, Father Keenan and, of course, Father Grace. Many of them are dead now, but they have left at least one of their charges with a lot of kindly and grateful memories.

My school days, however, did not end with distinction. My Intermediate results were so bad that my father decided that one more year would be sufficient before a major decision was made. Declan, who was two years behind me, took one look at my Intermediate results, allowed himself to consider the consequences of a similar result for himself, and promptly announced that he would be more than happy to betake himself to Synge Street to complete his schooling. Everybody was quite pleased. I recall my father saying something to the effect, well at least that's one college fee less per annum. As it happens, Declan completed his schooling at Synge Street most successfully and got an extremely good Leaving Certificate result.

I found fifth year a most pleasant experience indeed. Not as much was expected of me anymore, and even Father Devane, who had tried in vain to teach me maths, had more or less given up on the job. Father Devane had become especially disillusioned when, on the last day of school before we went in to do our 'Inter', he encountered myself and Squeaky O'Kelly in deep conversation in the back row of the class. Squeaky, who had a head of lank brown hair, had the remarkable ability of being able to move his scalp in such a way that his fringe would cover his nose, while his ears moved in a circular motion at the same time. He was teaching me how to do this (with some success, I might add; I am now able to perform that interesting if useless little feat, minus the fringe of course). Father Devane, however, could not be told precisely what was under discussion, so I decided I would tell him that Mr O'Kelly was kindly bringing me up to date on where our geometry course ended. In other words, which was the final proposition I should memorise before the exam. Father Devane was quite restrained in his reaction, though obviously incredulous.

'You don't know where the course ends?' he said. 'And this is your final day?'

He was right, of course. My results, in single figures – percentage-wise that is – proved that I hadn't absorbed a great deal. Trigonometry was another one of his courses, but when I received my big red trigonometry book at the beginning of third year I opened it up, wrote my name in it, glanced at all those indecipherable symbols and closed it, never to open it again. When the book was passed on to Declan years later, the pages were still stuck together.

Anyway, I completed fifth year playing good rugby, winning a few medals at athletics, playing soccer in the AUL minor league and featuring in one of the school plays. They were the good bits. The bad bit arrived at the end of the year, in the form of my school report, which showed that, if anything, I had regressed during the course of the twelve months. This was too much for my father. He promptly took me to the principal of the Rathmines Technical School and asked him would he take me on and maybe let me do the Matriculation Exam. The principal said I would need to do a short, easy entrance test, to which I nodded enthusiastically. A few days later, the principal asked my father to come in for a little chat. He told him that I had failed the exam. But not just failed; I had failed in a very spectacular way. He told my father that he didn't think there was really much point in me continuing with my academic studies, that in fact I would really need to go back to the very beginning in some subjects and start all over again. Thus ended my collegiate years.

Fear and Loving in the Capital

During these years, my father had acquired a penchant for moving house. Why, I don't know. Perhaps he thought that moving house would change the atmosphere in the home; but, whatever the reason, move we did. We moved from Hazelbrook Road to Ashfield Road in Ranelagh, from whence Declan and I would cycle every day to Terenure College. No mean feat for anybody who knows the distance – about four miles – all uphill, for those who don't. We also had a short spell in Terenure, in an apartment, or a flat, as it was called then.

We were evidently waiting to move into a new house, because there were a number of short stops during that particular year. From Terenure we moved out to Bray. My father used to drop us to school, and Declan and I experienced the less than appetising dinners that the boarders were treated to. From Bray we moved down to Tramore in County Waterford, where my father had some family connections, and, as this was during the summer, we were able to while away a good deal of the summer months in the dunes and on the beach.

We spent most of our holidays in Tramore when we were growing up and we knew the place and loved it very much. When Declan and

I were very young, about eleven and nine respectively, we went climbing the cliffs in Tramore. Our parents had sent the two of us down to stay with friends of theirs for a couple of weeks. We were with two of our own friends, the Pierce brothers from Castlecomer, and I was forever encouraging Declan to climb cliffs and do vaguely dangerous things of which my mother would greatly disapprove. So, here we were, climbing a quite tricky cliff in Tramore. I was on one side of the cliff with Michael Pierce and we were fairly close to the top. I knew that Declan and Tommy, who were on the other side of the cliff, were close to the top as well. Suddenly there was a scream, followed by the sound of something sliding and crashing down the cliff.

Tommy shouted, 'Declan's fallen!'

I don't know how I got down that cliff, but, when I did, I found Declan lying between two jagged rocks with his leg obviously seriously damaged – a bit of bone was protruding from it. It's all somewhat hazy now, but I remember my turmoil at the time. An ambulance was called and men came with a stretcher, took him from the base of the cliff and brought him to a hospital in Waterford. I was scared out of my wits and very confused. I had Declan's shoe under my arm and I walked off on my own, hiding in the cliffs and bays out towards the Metal Man. My mother and father were notified in Dublin of the accident and came down to Tramore immediately. Having visited Declan in hospital, they went looking for me.

For my part, I couldn't find the courage to face the music until after midnight that night. I must have cut a pretty forlorn figure, sloping in the door of the guest-house, clutching Dec's shoe to my chest. My father and mother were frantic with worry and there were search parties and police out around the resort looking for me. As it happened, Declan was fine in time. His collarbone had been broken and later he was left with a couple of bad scars on his leg and a slight squint in one eye. He never came climbing cliffs with me again.

Anyway, we returned from Tramore to move into our brand new

house in Fortfield, back in Terenure, and close to the Terenure College back entrance.

My parents' relationship was deteriorating all the while. For years now the tension had simply become a part of our home life. I assumed the older brother role and tried to protect Declan and the others as much as possible from the moods and black humours which were a daily feature of our lives. Invariably, when my father had a few drinks too many, a bad row would develop. He was, by now, spending most of his day at the garage – he would leave at ten in the morning, come back for his dinner or lunch for three-quarters of an hour or so, then return to the garage. He would come home for his tea at around six and then go back and serve petrol until, say, ten, and see out the rest of the evening in the pub until closing time.

He was a fairly heavy drinker – not a drunk, but fond of a drink. When these rows occurred, I would wrap myself in a blanket and sit on the stairs listening. If it threatened to become violent, I would rush into the kitchen shouting and screaming at my father, trying to break it up. I would be ushered up to bed by my mother, who would then, of course, return to the fray using my intervention as ammunition. Declan would try to sit with me on the stairs, but I would threaten him with all sorts of injuries and deprivations until he went back to bed.

I remember those nights with great pain and anger. I knew my parents had dreadful problems in their marriage, but I didn't know whether this was the norm. I couldn't, or wouldn't, speak to my friends about it. I never spoke to anyone about these problems, except my own brothers and sisters. It was very hard on them. Declan was a lovely, affable child who hero-worshipped me. I truly don't know what I was like in those days, but I believe that I was often sharp, argumentative, hostile.

While my mother called my father a 'street angel and a house devil', I would pretend to my friends that everything was just fine at home. All my friends thought my mother was great, but were wary of my father's moodiness, which seldom abated. One evening, after a number of my pals had been in the house, I challenged him and told him that if he ever again treated any of my friends as badly as he had that evening, I would leave the house. He didn't take me at all seriously and subsequently told my mother that my face, when I was giving out to him, was all scrunched up 'like a sixpence'.

There was, however, one particularly dreadful night. After a terrible row, which I had helped break up, my mother went sobbing to bed. My father was sitting on his own in the kitchen when I came back down. I closed the door behind me, picked up the bread knife and told him I would prefer he was dead. He said nothing, he just looked at me.

He said, 'What are you going to do with that knife?'

'I don't know.'

There was a pause. Suddenly I drew the knife back and threw it as hard as I could at him. He flung himself to one side and the knife stuck fast in the back door, where it quivered in the silence. We were both shocked. I didn't say a word, I just turned away and went to bed. After an hour or so, when I didn't hear him going upstairs, I went down to the kitchen. He was sitting in his chair, silently crying. He didn't say anything and I couldn't think of anything to say to him, so, once again, I turned and went to bed. I was no more than fourteen, maybe fifteen, at the time. Many times since have I thought of that night, often in the context of my own beloved son, Mark, who, as I write, is eighteen years of age. I think with horror of how I would have felt had Mark, at the age of fourteen, tried to knife me. Neither my father nor anybody else ever spoke to me about that incident afterwards.

I truly hated my father through those years, with the hatred of the young, the spirited, the immature. He never, to my knowledge, tried to make me feel otherwise and it was only many years later, when I began to have some degree of success on TV and radio, that we managed to cobble together some kind of superficial relationship.

How much of this unhappiness was my father's fault and how much my mother's, I will never know. My mother certainly created mischief in the house. She constantly complained about her poor health – she was frequently ill with migraines or 'nerves' – and always, in some manner or form, its cause found its way back to my father. Night after night she would talk to her children, singly or in groups, about the sadness of her marriage, her poor health, and about the things that we must watch out for in the future when we chose a partner. John recalls Ma keeping him up all night, 'giving out' about Da, and then his cycling to school the next day having had no sleep.

I don't want to be too hard on my mother, because in many ways she was a quite exceptional woman. She was small, feisty and strong-willed. She was ahead of her time in her liberal views; deeply religious, yes, but also willing to help out those who had in some way transgressed against society. She was kind to unmarried mothers, as they were known then, understanding of those in financial difficulties and good to older people. She was also a hugely formative influence on the lives of her children. From very early days, she inculcated into all of us a spirit of adventure, a culture of 'why not', a belief that all things are possible if you will only try.

'Michael,' she told me, 'Always remember, the best education you can have in your life is travel. God made a huge and wonderful world and it's your duty to see as much of it as you can in your lifetime.'

She instilled in me a love of variety, a belief in my own abilities and an openness of mind. And she did the same for Declan, Pat, Catherine and John. Gretta, her older sister, said to me recently that my mother would have made a wonderful army general. She knew how to make people respond to her, and she knew how to get her own way. She was a manipulator – sometimes positively, sometimes harmfully.

There was an occasion in Fortfield when my mother was ill with a streptococcal throat. I was about twelve at the time. It was late in the evening and and her throat was getting progressively worse. Declan and I were literally kneeling around the bed, looking out the window regularly, waiting for Da to come home so he could call the doctor. We didn't have a telephone at the time and Ma, for her own reasons, wouldn't let us go out for a doctor, so we waited and waited. She seemed to be deteriorating at a rapid pace – she was gagging and choking and barely conscious. Yet she wouldn't permit either of us to go out of the room. She kept saying, 'Your father will be here soon.' But, of course, he didn't arrive. I recall looking out of the window for hours that evening in a welter of fear, panic and anger.

I was convinced she was going to die, and so, it seemed, was she, because she did refer to the possibility that Da might need to get a priest as well. When eventually he came home, 'well on' as they say, after the pub, I attacked him at the hall door and told him that Ma was dying upstairs and where the hell was he until now and he'd better go and get a doctor. He said nothing, went upstairs, saw Ma, came down and started making a cup of tea.

'Sit down there, Michael,' he said to me. I sat at the table, glaring at him.

'I want you to know something,' he said. 'If your mother dies tonight, it will be your fault.'

Why he said it, I don't know – probably because of the viciousness of my attack on him when he came into the house – but I was shattered. I remember spending most of the night sitting outside her bedroom, wrapped in a blanket, listening to her breathing, checking to see that she was still alive. I suppose it seems poignant, even funny, at this remove, but these were desperately emotional times for me.

My mother insisted we kiss her on the cheek when we came into the house, when we went out of the house and when we were going to bed. She liked to believe that she was loved and cherished by her children. And we did love her, and we did cherish her, and we did try to protect her. And in so doing we further alienated our father. Why didn't he make some effort to redress the balance, why didn't he fight his paternal corner, why didn't he tell us he wanted some of our time, of our affection even? Perhaps he felt that, if he asked for some affection from us, it would mean he would have to give some back, and he couldn't, or wouldn't, do that. Why didn't he point out some of my mother's peccadilloes, try to justify his behaviour, try to give himself more stature in our eyes? It saddens me that I'll never know the answer to these questions. But I do believe that they were two good, vulnerable, highly individualistic, utterly incompatible people who almost destroyed each other's, and their children's, lives.

In time, the family began to disperse. Declan was first to go, at the age of seventeen, then I went and the burden fell upon the other members of the family: Pat, the eldest girl, who has a similar personality to my own and who also used to try to protect Catherine; Catherine, who would make angry faces at my father during mealtimes when he wasn't looking; and John, the youngest, always contained and quiet. John had a bad time. Ma relied on him a lot and Da, in later years, began to play on his good nature. John was, and is, kind, willing to help people, quiet, unemotional and non-committal. And I recall him as a child sitting in total and abject silence during mealtimes.

When I was about sixteen, my mother had a nervous breakdown. She was sent to St Edmundsbury's in Lucan for treatment. I don't know how serious her breakdown was. She had always told us that she suffered from her nerves, but we never knew quite how serious the problem was. She was there for a number of months and seemed to be responding well.

During that time, we, the children, visited her twice or three times a week, but my father visited her every single day. They would sit in near total silence for a short period of time and then he would leave. She would give him a peck on the cheek, say, 'Thank you, Jack, for visiting,' and off he would go.

One evening, two or three months into this period, when there was no sign of my mother making any move to come home, we went *en famille* to visit her. As usual, she told us she wasn't feeling well at all and that the doctors were very concerned about her, and, as usual, we forebore from telling her how well she looked. Such a comment was guaranteed to get a very chilly reception indeed. Anyway, she was sitting in a chair in her room, wearing her overcoat, which struck us as strange; she was also wearing make-up. The room seemed to us to be very warm, but we didn't say anything. She seemed anxious for us to leave and so, not wishing to outstay our welcome, we got up to go. We left, went down to the hall, and my father decided that he had better go into the office and make some enquiries about my mother and why she should be feeling the cold so badly.

The rest of us waited outside of the office in a sort of alcove. Next minute we heard feet rushing down the marble corridor and looked up to see Ma flying past at a rate of knots, her coat opening to reveal her good green party dress. We followed behind, all five of us, and saw her board a coach with a number of other people and drive off. We made a few tentative inquiries and discovered that there was a dance in the Spa Hotel every week and some of the healthier patients were permitted to go. We told Da about the miraculous recovery and he grinned rather ruefully and said that maybe she needed to stay another few weeks to improve her steps. For over a week we abided by our pact not to mention it to her, but eventually I could resist it no longer. I asked her would she be going to the dance this week. There was a long painful silence before she told us that the doctors were insisting that she get out into the world on a gradual basis, and see how her nerves would stand it. She was home within the week.

Meanwhile, we still had not finished moving. From Fortfield we moved to Brighton Avenue in Rathgar, where Declan and I became quite proficient at tennis in the Aer Lingus Tennis Club. It was here that I enjoyed my first fumbling and bumbling experiences with members of the opposite sex. Kathleen Doyle was my first girlfriend, followed by Noreen Curran, whose brother John could be heard practising clarinet and saxophone right across the tennis courts of Brighton Square. John is now, of course, one of the country's top musicians.

Then there was Grace O'Shaughnessy, who went on to be Europe's Ideal Woman and who currently features in the TV programme, *Live at Three.* I was sitting on a bench in the square one summer afternoon with my arm around Grace, kissing her passionately, as I thought at the time – though it was probably a sad little peck on the ear – when I looked up and, through a gap in the hedge, saw my mother looking at me. She had previously caught me in a bare-faced lie when she asked me how I had enjoyed the movies at the Classic Cinema with Liam O'Gorman and I had told her how exciting it was, only to be informed that she knew 'damn well' I had been with Noreen Curran and that I had paid for Noreen with her, my mother's, money. So I was pretty upset at being caught with Grace.

Grace understood my predicament perfectly and arrived at our house that evening at teatime to explain to my mother that she had had a fly in her ear and that I was trying to pick it out for her (with my *tongue?*) My mother was not as receptive as she might have been to Grace's little tale of truth and honour, particularly as I had, only fifteen minutes previously, confessed to my mother that, yes, I was, in fact, kissing Grace.

It was in Brighton Square that I went to the first of the few dances I attended during my teenage years. The Viscounts performed here, Tommy Ellis, John Curran, Jimmy McKay, and Billy Butler, I believe. They became a very successful band in subsequent years. Paul Russell was their lead singer and a major figure of glamour and talent to all of us at that stage. He also went on to perform regularly on that new medium, television. Television at that time seemed to us to consist of cricket matches viewed in black and white through a blanket of fog.

I hated these dances from the beginning, for one reason and one reason alone: I couldn't bear to see the girls on one side and the boys on the other, with the boys having their pick of the girls and the girls unable to reciprocate except in the Ladies' Choice. I would look at those young women done up in their taffeta and tulle and ponytails, chatting gaily to each other, apparently totally unconcerned, while the boys eyed them up and down, walked in their general direction, and invariably asked the girl beside them to dance while the first girl tried to keep a frown of disappointment from crossing her face. I found myself asking some of the plainer girls to dance, because I couldn't bear the thought of them going home to their parents later that night pretending they had had a wonderful night and had met some lovely boys. Of course, I knew many of the girls there and I was keen on some of them, but, because of my sad solicitude for everybody else's feelings, I was leaving gaps in my own relationships for other young 'gallants' to slip into!

I attended some dances in Aer Lingus and, later, a few more in Templeogue Tennis Club, before I abandoned the process entirely. My friends used to try to cajole me to go along with them, but I wouldn't. I simply couldn't stand the tension.

For most of my teenage years, I was fairly influential among my peers. I had pretty definite ideas about what I liked, I was good at sports and had a lot of interests. I loved books, music and films, and my rather dramatic gesture of refusing to go to any dances was, in fact, emulated by a number of my friends who would ask me, 'What are you doing tonight, anyway?' and would then say, 'Well, I think I'll go with you. I don't feel like going to the dance either.'

My mother tried to get me to learn the piano, but I flatly refused, I wasn't going to waste time with all those lessons. Declan, however, agreed to learn and became a very good pianist. But I bought records whenever I could. The first was Mel Tormé's 'Mountain Greenery'. This was closely followed by Elvis Presley's 'Heartbreak Hotel' and 'Hound Dog', Frankie Lynam and the Teenagers' 'Why Do Fools Fall in Love?', Guy Mitchell's 'Singin' the Blues', and so on. I used to lock myself into the dining-room, and sing along with all my heart and all my pent-up emotions.

Musicals of the time were *Hit the Deck*, *The Student Prince* and *Seven Brides for Seven Brothers*. Rhonda Fleming was the most beautiful creature you could imagine, but not as beautiful as Ann Sheridan. Poor Ann could only be seen in black and white, whereas Rhonda's red hair came up so beautifully in colour. Susan Hayward was another big favourite, but she was always either drunk or being gassed in prison, so she was just a little too dramatic for a real relationship. And then along came Kim Novak. She was the ultimate. How was I to know that she was of questionable sexual orientation, was a 'nut' for animals, was reputed to have actually 'had it off' with Richard Johnson during a love scene for a movie, and was a total recluse? I loved her so much, I wanted her to be my mother. All arched eyebrows, low-cut dresses, husky voice and short blond hair. Everybody's typical ideal mother!

The Green Cinema was a favourite on the afternoons when we were 'mitching' from school, because it only cost fourpence to get in. I recall one memorable afternoon when three of us were sitting in the cinema as the lights came up. One of our number turned and saw Mr O'Connell, our English teacher, sitting just behind us. Mr O'Connell smiled at us, waved, and told us how much he was looking forward to seeing us in school the next morning. It made for a pretty tense evening, I can tell you.

Big Julie Gets Stabbed

After my schooldays had been involuntarily terminated, I was, as was said at the time, 'put into the drapery'. My father was bitterly disappointed that neither myself nor Declan had the slightest interest in following him into the motor business. By now he owned the Harold's Cross garage, right beside the greyhound track, and was leasing the Greenmount petrol station, which was near Harold's Cross bridge. Despite our protestations, Declan and I used to spend the summer months serving petrol in both places. In actual fact, we quite enjoyed it and found it handy for making a few extra bob for films and records.

My father always seemed to be fond of Declan, but he had very little time for his eldest pride and joy, so when I told him, in no uncertain terms, that I didn't like engines and frankly had no interest in the slightest in how they worked – and, besides, found it quite draughty working in the garage – he made different plans for me.

Among his larger customers was Crowe Wilson's, a major wholesale drapery in Lower Bridge Street in the centre of Dublin. Through his connections, he found me a job as an apprentice draper and, although

I began the job with some misgivings, I found that I adapted very quickly to this new lifestyle. I cycled every morning from our latest and, as it turned out, our final family home in Vernon Grove, Rathgar, into Crowe Wilson's, where I joined the other apprentices at the post table. First thing in the morning every day, all the apprentices from the different departments gathered to sift through the orders which had been posted in by our customers around the country, and each apprentice took the requisite orders for his department. We would occasionally bolster Mr Lewis's order – he being the 'boots' buyer – by including an order for a single pair of women's blue interlocking knickers to go with the seven pairs of hobnail boots, size nine and a half, that were on the order. The 'initiation' ceremony for a new apprentice involved being sent around the building asking for the 'glass hammer' or the '4-foot yardstick'.

Our ambitions were minimal: we all aspired to one day becoming Mr Gilbert, who was the buyer of the ladies' outfitting department. Mr Gilbert, who was small and dapper with a Gilbert Roland moustache, earned one thousand pounds a year and drove a Morris Minor – his own. This, to us, was the big-time. We were currently earning in the region of seventeen and sixpence a week each, so this became my major ambition – to one day earn a thousand pounds a year and, perhaps, if my good fortune held, to buy a Morris Minor just like Mr Gilbert's.

I started in the haberdashery department, where I spent most of the day cutting oilskin into tablecloths, then I graduated to Mr Gilbert's department, where he promptly corrected me for overuse of the word 'okay'.

Some months later I was transferred to my final home, the hosiery department, under the legendary Mr Armstrong. Mr Armstrong, his chargehand Mr Flood and his assistant Mr Campbell were renowned for being impossible to work with. Mr Armstrong was a small, ruddy Northerner with a short temper, Mr Campbell, also a Northerner, was tall and ruddy with an even shorter temper and Mr Flood was a sarcastic Dubliner who tolerated his Northern colleagues with detached cynical amusement. They were all quite elderly. After a fairly shaky start, I managed to fit in quite beautifully.

Mr Armstrong would send me on messages to get him a certain kind of soup, Mr Flood would make an occasional kind comment about my speed around the department and Mr Campbell once looked at me over his half-rimmed glasses and informed me that if I kept making such rapid progress I, too, could one day become a member of the Railway Union Bowling Club!

I had a facility for keeping a mental record of the stock of the department. Mr Armstrong would occasionally invite other buyers into the department and throw questions at me about how many Sun Frolic Nylon Hose sized nine we had in stock, or how many green Fair Isle sweaters were left, and I would give him answers that curiously enough were as often as not correct. He would send me scurrying away to confirm my answers and, with a theatrical flourish, would claim he had the best apprentice in the building. I was in my element. I could do the work in my sleep, and one day Mr Armstrong told me that in a very short while I was likely to be the 'youngest Assistant Draper ever in the history of Crowe Wilson's'. I smiled, stuttered, mumbled and felt the distant stirring of misgivings. Did I wish to remain in the drapery? Did I want to stay in Crowe Wilson's? Did I even want a Morris Minor?

My father had by this time received good reports about my progress and so I felt I might take advantage of the slight change in his attitude towards me by asking him if he could find me something a little more interesting. Within a matter of weeks, I found myself in the Castrol Oil Company, smack in the centre of Terenure, where I began my less than illustrious career as Office Boy.

I wasn't a success. I found the work boring, tedious and repetitive and the idea of sending out invoice after invoice and licking envelopes deeply unpleasant. Also I knew that Mr Metcalf, the office manager, didn't like me. Mr Metcalf was a tall, stiff, upright, bald man, who I think was a Mormon and who was possessed of two piercing blue eyes which bored into me as I sat at my desk, fumbling. Mr Metcalf's glass office was directly behind my desk and he had an uninterrupted view of his entire staff. He had no sense of humour whatsoever. He always wore a grey suit. In fact he wore grey everything – he even drove a grey car. Anyway, I knew that my days with Mr Metcalf were numbered.

By this stage I was doing a bit of acting. The Dublin Shakespeare Society, an amateur dramatic society in a basement in Fitzwilliam's Square, had sought me out after school and invited me to join. This was based on some of the performances they had seen me give in Terenure, where I must have seemed like adequate fodder for their productions. So I went down to the basement and auditioned, and was promptly invited to play Laertes in their forthcoming production of *Hamlet*.

At this stage, of course, I was still playing rugby and had been promoted to the Past Pupils' Team, where I was playing quite well. However, during the course of one of the matches, an opposing player decided that he would teach me a thing or two about forward play. He was an interprovincial wing forward, about twenty-eight years of age, weighing around fourteen stone. I was seventeen years of age, a fairly useful schools player, but only weighing about ten stone, so the pairing was uneven. By half-time I had acquired a broken nose and three broken ribs, and the referee had forbidden me to emerge for the second half. So, for the time being, acting took over as a priority.

That production of *Hamlet* proved to be a most effective learning process for me. I enjoyed the part of Laertes and seem to have been fairly useful in the role. We entered a number of festivals and to our amazement we won the Newry Drama Festival and thereby qualified for the All-Ireland Amateur Drama finals in Athlone. As a result of winning Newry, we were invited to stage *Hamlet* in the old Belfast Opera House and we were more than happy to oblige. This was to be the scene of what I later considered to be the finest 'ad lib' I have ever witnessed in a performance of Shakespeare.

Kevin Redmond, who was playing Claudius, and Patricia Bailey, playing Gertrude, were on-stage having a meaningful verbal interchange, at the end of which Kevin had to go to downstage right and call Rosencrantz and Guildenstern. This he did. Rosencrantz and Guildenstern were, according to the script, expected to enter immediately. Unfortunately, Rosencrantz and Guildenstern were at that moment up seven flights of stairs in their dressing-room on the top floor of the opera house, playing cards. Kevin went back to the centre of the stage, made some movements with his shoulders which suggested irritation or exasperation, and came back downstage right to call again, a little more forcefully, 'Ho, Rosencrantz, Guildenstern.' Still no response. By this time there was some panic off-stage, with Father O'Donohue, the play's producer, running up the stairs himself, bellowing for 'those two bastards' and threatening them with all kinds of non-secular physical indignities when he got his hands on them.

Meanwhile, on-stage, Kevin and Patricia were looking a little edgy and the audience was rattling its collective sweet papers, wondering was this theatrical licence or could there possibly be a problem? Kevin ventured downstage right once more and, a little tremulously this time, called again for the two gents in question. Again no response. He then seemed to make a decision. He walked back to centre stage, where Gertrude was kneeling upon her four-poster, and announced, while looking out over the audience's heads, 'Aha! Methinks I see the sun come o'er yonder hill. I must away.' He nodded abruptly to Gertrude and, with full magisterial bearing, exited down right.

As soon as he was off-stage, he roared, if it is possible to roar in a stage whisper, 'Where's those two fuckers? I'll fucking kill them!' Whereupon Rosencrantz and Guildenstern, looking somewhat abashed and not a little flustered, came crashing down the stairs with Father O'Donohue in hot pursuit. All went back onto the stage and continued the scene.

We were not such a success at the All-Ireland finals in Athlone, however. In fact, we finished last. John Fernald, who was the director of the Royal Academy of Dramatic Art in London – or RADA, as it was known – was the adjudicator and he was quite fulsome in his praise of Paddy Finegan, who played Hamlet, but even more fulsome in his praise of the young actor who played the part of Laertes! I was pleased, embarrassed and delighted when, later that evening, Mr Fernald sought me out and invited me to accept a scholarship to RADA. I thanked him very much and said that I would most certainly consider it and gave him my address and details. He subsequently wrote to me inviting me to go, but I really wasn't that interested in getting down to the truly serious business of acting at that stage, so I ignored his letter.

I remained with the Dublin Shakespeare Society for a few years, although it was the source of one of the more embarrassing incidents of my theatrical career. I was cast as Cassius in *Julius Caesar* and the aforementioned Kevin Redmond, who was a fine actor, was playing Caesar. When it came to the assassination scene, Kevin, as Caesar, was seated on a fairly large throne with big wooden arms. He placed both his hands on the arms, with his elbows raised to accommodate the stabbing by his assassins.

As with many such amateur productions, we were clad in various styles and periods. One assassin had forgotten to take off his wristwatch; another was wearing his bedroom slippers. Eamon Morrissey, who was playing Casca in the same production, had, when the soothsayer pulled his toga a little too hard and the toga fell around his ankles, revealed himself to be wearing his long woolly underpants and his interlock vest. The swords we were carrying had mostly not been invented yet. There were claymores, rapiers and sabres – so Caesar was not going to be short of a variety of stab wounds as he 'shed the mortal coil'.

Anyway, there we all were grouped around Caesar, just about to stab, when Brutus, played by Jack Riordan – a bigger, heavier man than I was – accidentally nudged me. As I stabbed with my rapier, my aim went slightly awry and the sword went straight into and through Kevin's left hand. Kevin was a bit taken aback. He looked at his hand, he looked at me, and, instead of saying 'Et tu, Brute' and expiring, he said 'Oh, Jesus Christ' and fainted – which was, in fact, historically inaccurate, as Jesus wasn't born until some years afterwards. I had to extricate my sword, with profuse apologies, from Kevin's hand and, sick with remorse, continue to act. It was easier for Kevin – he at least was 'dead'. *I* had to finish the rest of the play.

It was when I was cast as 'Romeo' that I realised that my association with the Dublin Shakespeare Society would inevitably end. I didn't want to play such a 'drippy' part and I didn't really want to be the Principal Boy at the 'Shakes', as it was popularly known. Besides, as soon as my photo appeared in the paper with the news that I was playing Romeo, my life at Castrol changed quite dramatically. The girls in the office, all of whom were older than me, made my life pretty difficult. It was 'Romeo, could you bring me a cup of coffee?', 'Romeo, could you sweeten my tea?', 'Romeo, how long can you hold a kiss for?' All that and more! I was young enough to be embarrassed and too young to take advantage of the situation.

By now I had begun to attend the Brendan Smith Academy of Acting in South Great George's Street. It was here that I met up with Tony Dwyer, who was to become a lifelong friend. Tony was later to act as my 'best man'. I enjoyed my two years in the Academy, and became Chairman of the Students' Union, as well as winning the 'best actor' award in each of the years I was there.

There were some interesting people at the Academy at that time. I recall Emmet Bergin, who was then a seventeen-year-old Marlon Brando look-alike in a black leather jacket, white T-shirt and jeans. Emmet is now, of course, a fine actor and has found fame as 'Dick' in *Glenroe*. At that time he had a very pronounced Dublin accent and Brendan Smith found it difficult to find suitable roles for him. Emmet spent years working on his voice and accent, and now it is as well-modulated as you could possibly wish!

There was the young, sprightly and, even then, somewhat 'posh'

Terry Keane. Terry always had a sophisticated air about her and she didn't mix easily with most of the other students, but she and I struck up quite a rapport when we were cast opposite each other in *The Importance of Being Earnest*. Somehow, I don't think Terry ever expected to find herself cast as Pegeen Mike, but I think she was pleased to feature in a Wilde play where one carried a parasol with panache and wore a pretty bonnet and flouncing crinolines.

One of our instructors at the time was Brendan O'Reilly, who had recently returned from an athletic scholarship in Michigan and who was lecturing on this new-fangled invention – television. He made up three little cardboard boxes on pedestals and we all pretended they were cameras and read scripts into them, trying not to either feel or appear too foolish as we did so. Brendan impressed us mightily with his comprehensive knowledge of television, but then, since we believed the cardboard boxes were cameras, we were obviously prepared to believe anything he told us. One of the most delightful and charming of men, Brendan became legendary, later, in the RTE sports department, for the apparent casualness of his approach to sports announcing. He would leave it late to come into studio and on many occasions, I recall, the signature tune was playing while Brendan ran in the door. On one occasion, to teach him a lesson, the camera crew decided to play a joke on him. They simply removed his chair. Brendan ran into the studio at the appointed time – while the signature tune was playing, naturally – to find that there was no chair, so he was forced to read the sports results crouching at the desk.

Brendan Smith, a small, rotund, humorous man with a very powerful personality, had, as well as founding the only acting academy in Dublin city, initiated the Dublin Theatre Festival and was on his way to becoming the owner of the Olympia Theatre. He was a formidable man and I was quite flattered when he invited me to join his summer repertory company at Butlin's Mosney. This was an annual enterprise for which he gathered some professional and some semi-professional actors.

When I started, there were people like Brendan Cauldwell, Martin Dempsey, Jim Nealon, Iris Lawlor, my old friend Eamon Morrissey, Pat Nolan, Brendan's wife Beryl Fagan, Jacqueline Ryan, Aidan Grennell, and many more. It was tremendous fun and very good experience. Fun, because of the practical jokes that people used to play on each other to break the monotony of performing plays in front of quarter-full halls, with the action continually interrupted by the Tannoy system reminding the audience that there was 'a baby crying' in, if not their own, certainly an adjoining chalet. There was the night I was playing a garda and had to make a dramatic exit. I picked up my hat from the table, where it had lain since the previous act. Somebody, however, had filled it with frozen peas. So, as I raised it to my head, I was showered with peas, which bounced noisily all over the stage and into the auditorium.

Actor in Heavenly Orbit

I t was Mr Smith (never 'Brendan' to his minions) who suggested that I might like to consider theatre as a full-time profession. By then, I was actually receiving offers of employment from professional theatre companies. Mr Smith suggested he would assist my transformation from the world of commerce by offering me a position as assistant to Dick Condon, who was the administrator of the Dublin Theatre Festival. Eamon Morrissey was already *in situ* as assistant administrator so I became 'assistant assistant' administrator. To augment the inordinately meagre income proposed by Mr Smith, he suggested I might like to work for Adrian Cronin, who at that time was running Radio Publicity Limited. This company was set up by Brendan Smith and John McConnell of McConnell's Advertising as the radio arm of the burgeoning McConnell's business. It was Radio Publicity's function to script and produce all of McConnell's sponsored radio programmes. With relief, I handed in my notice at Castrol and embarked on a great new adventure.

My mother was extremely supportive, telling me that whatever I wanted to do was fine by her. My father turned darkly into his early evening fry. So here I was, eighteen years of age, involved in the early days of the Dublin Theatre Festival. I found myself writing scripts for the Colgate–Palmolive and Lemon's sponsored programmes and doing a bit of acting in my spare time. It was pretty heady stuff.

Part of my job spec at the time was to carry the tin of records and scripts down to Radio Éireann's studios in the GPO in Henry Street every Monday and Thursday lunchtime for the Colgate–Palmolive programme, which went out 'live' on those days, presented by Beryl Fagan, Brendan Smith's wife, and Frank Purcell, an architect who was blessed with a fine and rounded voice.

It was here that I first encountered the young Gay Byrne, dapper, cocky, well dressed, a young man (although a good few years older than myself) on his way to somewhere that even he hadn't quite defined. Or had he? He was known by the programme and technical staff in Radio Éireann to be extremely ambitious, even believing he was good enough to get work in England, for God's sake!

I recall asking Gay to come into Peter Hunt's studios on one occasion to record a pilot programme for Lyons' Tea. He graciously agreed. I had come up with a device, quite new then, of fading the introductory music of a record under the voice of the presenter so that the singer commenced the song as the presenter finished speaking. I did this with Gay for his first record and, when the record was playing, I asked him what did he think? He looked at me fairly disparagingly and said he thought it wasn't bad. As it happens, we didn't get the contract and so I didn't have the pleasure of working on a long-term basis with Gay at that stage.

The Dublin Theatre Festival office was a hilarious place to work. Dick Condon, who went on to become one of the most innovative theatre managers in these islands when he took over the Theatre Royal in Norwich, was a joy to work with. He had a tremendous sense of fun and mischief, and of course Morrissey and myself were the perfect acolytes. There were practical jokes to be played – and if there was fun to be had, we found it. And, of course, we loved being involved in the

Theatre Festival and all the paraphernalia that went with it. It was actually Dick who did all the work and we knew he would eventually sort out the problems we created for him.

At this time I was doing a strong line with an attractive blonde girl named Colette Kavanagh. Colette now runs her own extremely successful textile business in Amsterdam. I was madly in love with Colette when Brendan Smith asked me if I would like to accompany the Dublin Festival Company on their eight-week European tour as assistant stage manager. Naturally, I couldn't but accept such an exotic offer.

The plays we were to stage were by George Bernard Shaw: *Mrs Warren's Profession* and *Candida*. The star of the show was Eithne Dunne, the director was her husband, Gerald Healy, and among the cast were Liam Gaffney, Desmond Jordan and that lovely couple, David Kelly and Laurie Morton, who were in fact using the tour as their honeymoon. I was the 'baby' of the company and was looked after and treated as such by the older members of the cast. But I learned a lot about life on that tour.

On the first night out, one of the lady members invited me to her room and attempted to have her way with me. The seduction was rudely interrupted by the Dutch coach driver, who had arrived at the room with a bottle of wine and the express intention of doing to her what she was attempting to do to me. I, mightily confused in any case, took the opportunity to retreat to my own room.

Our tour took us from Holland to Luxemburg, Belgium, Germany, Norway, Sweden, Denmark, and home. During its course I fell head-over-heels in love with a rather wild young woman who was part of the company. We became extremely close, despite my guilty qualms about Colette. One night I returned to our hotel and, as I walked along the corridor towards my room, her door opened and she emerged: tall, lissome, graceful – and naked. At exactly that moment the manager of the hotel turned the corner at the far end of the corridor, saw me walking towards this naked woman and promptly informed both of us that we were to leave the hotel post-haste.

I must mention that, although there had been some casual kissing and fumbling, no real intimacy had taken place between the dashing damsel and myself. So this expulsion from the Garden of Delight only heightened my sense of romantic destiny. If my love was greeting me in such a manner so late at night, then surely many pleasures lay ahead for me. And so our 'romance' continued. She gave me a beautiful photo of herself, inscribed with 'all my love'. She even washed my shirt and gave me a tie (striped) for my birthday.

The romance lasted until one fateful night in Copenhagen. As we sat in a small intimate bar with some of the other members of the cast, my beloved excused herself and went and sat on a bar stool beside another female member of our group. A good deal of drink had been taken and it was with some consternation that I noticed my amour slip her hand up the back of the other woman's blouse, surreptitiously open her bra, and slide her free hand down the front to fondle the exposed breasts. I nearly choked on my pink gin (I was experimenting with drinks at the time and was determined to try them all; not necessarily at the same time, of course). Here was the love of my life and she was a 'lezzer'! It wasn't me she had been waiting for naked that night, weeks earlier. It was this other woman – I mean, this woman. I was soon assured, when my stricken expression was noticed, that this little affair had been going on ever since the tour began.

In Brussels, too, my education was extended. On a beautiful afternoon, in a hotel which boasted a tennis court, I went to reception, got two tennis rackets and a few balls, came back upstairs and burst into the room of one of the younger male members of the cast with whom I had arranged a game of tennis. It took a moment for my eyes to adjust to the dim light, but, when they did, there was my erstwhile opponent *in flagrante delicto* with the wine waiter from the previous night. Not a stitch on either of them. Both of them on their knees and not a menu in sight. How I ever played another game of tennis, I'll never know!

Some time later, that same cast member invited me to his room for tea one evening. I went along, not at all apprehensive, as I was bigger and tougher than he was and, anyway, I quite enjoyed his company. He had brought his own Primus stove with him and he made us tea. One thing led to another – conversationally that is – and he began to tell me how he had become 'queer' (the word 'gay' was not a part of popular vocabulary then). He realised I had been shocked by the incident some days previously and he wanted to explain.

We sat in his room for most of the night while he talked. He recalled how, at the age of seven, he had felt different from other boys. He realised at an early stage that he had some feminine traits about him, that he was not attracted to women but he was attracted to men. It was a biological thing. Then came the darkness, the confusion and the awful dilemma of how to spend the rest of his life with such a secret. He could speak to neither family nor friends. There were only one or two options open to him. Firstly, he needed to get into a world that accommodated people such as himself; possibly the world of dance or theatre. So he started acting. Secondly, it was best that he didn't stay in Ireland, in case his secret got out. So he had moved to England.

I learned a great deal from that young man about people of a different sexual preference and I believe I learned to be tolerant and understanding long before it became fashionable to be liberal about such matters. When some of the other members of our group learned that I had spent most of the night in this man's room, they were scandalised. One or two actually verbally attacked him on the bus the next day, but I was able to reassure them that nothing whatsoever had happened and that we had simply had a very enjoyable chat.

When I returned to Dublin, I was a changed young man. My mother organised a little welcome home gathering for me, to which she invited Colette. She wouldn't permit me, however, to sit beside Colette, because we would 'only be holding hands and that sort of thing under the table', so my mother made me sit beside her. But I knew – and so did my mother, incidentally, as she told me later – that it was over between Colette and myself. Colette later reminded me, and I still blush to think of it, that, after breaking off the relationship with her a few nights later at her house, I walked down the road whistling. The stomach-churning shallowness of youth!

It was Beryl Fagan who suggested I should change my name to something that was more actor-ish. She thought that 'Michael Murphy' was a little too commonplace and I should choose a slightly more exotic name. I immediately thought of 'Rock Lancaster', but she said, no, just a small change in my own name.

'How about Mike Murphy?' she offered. 'I like the sound of that.'

I thought about it for a while, but I wasn't mad about it. At school I had been known mainly as 'Murph', and occasionally 'Mick', and I had grown quite used to these, but 'Mike' was something new. Still, it could have been worse and, for good or for ill, I asked Phyllis Ryan to put me down on the programme of *My Wife's Family* as 'Mike Murphy' and that was it. However, to this day, I am known to my family and friends as Michael, and, to some extent, I do regard Mike and Michael almost as separate entities.

By now I was in some demand as an actor. Barry Cassin had cast me in *My Wife's Family* at the Eblana, with Danny Cummins in the lead role. The same director cast me in Patrick Galvin's excellent play, *Cry the Believers*, also at the Eblana. This was a strong, meaty drama about a couple, played by Martin Dempsey and Anna Manahan, who were trapped in a difficult marriage, dominated by drink and rows, and the effect it had on their only son – me. I did pretty well in terms of critical reaction to my performances in these plays and, when Alan Simpson, the *enfant terrible* of his time, set about restaging his controversial *The Rose Tattoo*, he thought of me.

Simpson had already been brought to court and prosecuted for the first staging of this play in the Pike Theatre, and now he was testing the public's appetite and the government's liberality once again. He cast Anna Manahan and Pat Nolan in the main roles, myself as the sailor, and a young Dundalk actress named Eve Belton to play opposite me.

There was incredible public interest in the play – the theatre was booked out for weeks in advance and, when we opened, the reviews were uniformly good. But, again, it was not without controversy. It was not uncommon, during some of the performances, for members of the audience to walk out in high dudgeon. On one occasion, I recall playing my love scene down stage left with Eve Belton. Two middle-aged women got up noisily from their seats and began to make their way to the exit, which was right beside where Eve and I were standing. They were harrumphing and muttering as they made their way towards us. As they drew level, I departed totally from the script and addressed them directly.

'You're not leaving already?' I said, 'It's just getting to the best bit.'

There was, of course, a stunned reaction from the rest of the audience. The women weren't too sure whether I was still in character or not and then one or two members of the audience started to giggle. Eve went rigid with fear, all sensual thoughts banished momentarily from her mind, and then I continued with the scene. Phyllis Ryan, the producer, attacked me roundly afterwards, but I always felt that she was quite amused by the incident herself.

It was through *The Rose Tattoo* that I met my wife-to-be, Eileen Dixon. She was, at that time, employed as a secretary in Eamonn Andrews' studios. They produced sponsored programmes and staged shows and concerts. She was Fred O'Donovan's personal secretary, he being the managing director of the company, and she also was the great man, Eamonn Andrews', part-time secretary when he was in Dublin. Eileen and a girlfriend had booked well in advance for *The Rose Tattoo*, and it was a source of great amusement to both of us, through the years, that on the night before she came to the theatre she actually went to confession! She asked the priest to forgive her for what she was about to do – go to a 'dirty' play! He did, incidentally, oblige.

We met formally the following Sunday. Eileen had agreed to sell raffle tickets at a charity show in the Gaiety Theatre and I happened to be there. I remember seeing her in the downstairs bar of the Gaiety – tall, elegant, blue-eyed, smiling, simply glowing. I was instantly smitten. I asked Pat Nolan, my co-star in *The Rose Tattoo*, who had been speaking to her earlier, to introduce us, and he did. She remembered me well from the previous night and seemed a little shocked to be talking to such a wayward character as myself. From then on we were more or less inseparable.

Eventually, I plucked up courage and invited Eileen home to meet my parents. My father opened the door to her, and she told me later that, when he saw her, he said, 'My God, you took the sight right out of my eyes.' My mother wasn't quite so smitten – she immediately resented her. Eileen could play the piano brilliantly, could sew, was highly accomplished at embroidery and, of course, she was stunningly beautiful. My mother put as good a face on things as she could, but she never quite took to Eileen. She could see that she was destined in time to lose her eldest son, her warrior, to this interloper.

That night, my father was prevailed upon to drive Eileen home – I didn't have a car at the time – and in the course of the journey he advised her not to waste her time with me. He went on to say that I was a 'worthless bastard' and 'would never get anywhere'. She was deeply shocked when she told me about it the next day. I never spoke to him about it, I suppose because I considered what he said and decided there may just have been a grain of truth in it. But I never forgave him for saying it – ever.

Around that time I was cast in my first movie. *The Girl with Green Eyes*, Edna O'Brien's novel, had been adapted for the screen and was being shot in Dublin, starring Rita Tushingham, Peter Finch and Lynn Redgrave. I was auditioned for, and got, a small part. In my first scene, Abbey actor Pat Laffan and myself, in a grotty old van with two greyhounds in the back, had to drive to a house in Percy Place. I had then to get out of the van, walk up to the hall door and ring the bell. When Ms Tushingham – she of the huge, expressive eyes and the even larger expressive mouth – answered the door, I had to recite the memorable line: 'Howaya? Long time, no see.'

We had to do it a number of times, for various reasons, and it became a bit boring after a while, so I tried one or two variations. Eventually we got the scene in the can and we all sat around chatting, as people who are employed in movies do. I got on tremendously well with Lynn Redgrave, who was a tomboyish, humorous type, but Ms Tushingham was more introverted and took life extremely seriously. My suspicions that she may not have been altogether taken with me, either, were confirmed when I turned up for the second scene the next day. Ms Tushingham looked at me, and a slight cloud crossed her mobile features.

'Oh, is he here again?' she said. I knew then that the day's filming was not going to be easy. We were called upon, Ms Tushingham and myself, to sit in the Savoy cinema and 'neck', or 'coort' as the word was then, passionately. I found it extremely difficult. We were licking each other's ice cream and then kissing and nuzzling, but, every time the director called 'cut', Ms Tushingham took it upon herself to leap out of the chair, as if a mouse had nibbled her nylons.

Eventually we got the scene done and, when I saw it in the finished movie, it wasn't nearly as bad as I had thought it was going to be. She even looked as if she was enjoying the encounter, which shows what a damn good actress she is! And a damn fine person to boot! And I know she said the same about me!

Then there was the time Samuel Beckett came to see me in a play in Paris. Well . . . I may be exaggerating slightly, but he was there. Ulick O'Connor told me so, many moons later – and Ulick was with him. The play was *The Countess Cathleen* by W B Yeats. I was happy to go along as assistant stage manager, as well as portraying the 'angel' who appears to the peasants towards the end of the play. Jack McGowran, the legendary Beckett actor, was directing, and the Dublin Festival

Company were once again staging – Eithne Dunne, Ray McAnally, a rather nondescript little fellow from England whose name I don't recall playing the juvenile lead, Eamon Morrissey, Dermot Tuohy, and many other friends and acquaintances featured in lesser roles.

Brendan Smith was the impresario and he asked Jack McGowran to find a role for Brendan's wife, Beryl, so that she could have a week's break in Paris. Jack couldn't find a part for Beryl and so a compromise was reached. Beryl would appear before the show in a glittering evening dress, and, to harpist Maureen Hurley's accompaniment, would recite, for the benefit of the Parisian audience, a selection of Yeats's poetry. This would be the cultural introduction to the drama that was to follow. I, as the angel, prerecorded my speech in Peter Hunt's studios, so that they could superimpose echo and heavenly choirs. As much of my scene was in semi-darkness, it wasn't essential that I learn the speech by heart.

When we arrived in Paris, we found that we were all that had arrived – the cast and crew, that is – as the set had found its way to Berlin and wouldn't be in Paris in time for the show that evening. During the course of the day, a huge piece of orange gauze was found, which was hung at the back of the stage as a backdrop. But that was only the start. Among many other difficulties, there was now no rostrum of a suitable height for the angel to stand on for the big scene. Jack improvised. He told me that, during the blackout, before the angel was to appear, he himself would come on-stage with a chair, while I would carry out a small rostrum. I would place the rostrum on the stage, he would place the chair on top of that, and then I would climb up on the chair and from thence would deliver my heavenly speech.

That first night was not a success. As assistant stage manager, I was expected to act as 'prompter'. However, I had inadvertently gone missing for the very opening, which was of course Beryl's cultural introduction. What transpired was as follows. The lights went up to reveal a beaming Maureen Hurley *in situ*, fingers on strings, ready to play the harp. Beryl came on-stage from the opposite side looking radiant in her beautiful ball gown. She went to centre stage, curtsied to applause, moved slightly right and took up her speaking position. When the applause died down, she announced, '"The Wild Swans at Coole".'

Maureen Hurley waited patiently for the first line, but Beryl stood immobile. Maureen's smile became a little forced. Beryl seemed rigid in her posture. The audience became a little restless. Beryl inclined her head towards the wings; Maureen looked to her wings. The pause continued. Beryl had forgotten the first line of the poem!

After another unbearably long pause, Beryl quickly curtsied and very gracefully walked off in the direction from whence she had come. Maureen sat tense, no longer smiling, and remained thus until the lights blacked out.

I was coming in the stage door, having gone out to find Eamon Morrissey, when Dermot Tuohy met me and said, 'If I were you I'd stay out of Beryl's way for the next five days. She's going to have your guts for garters.' I cursed my luck. It would be my bad fortune to be missing just when Beryl forgot her lines. But, worse was to follow.

The play seemed to be going quite well, despite the absence of a set, when it came to my big moment. My costume consisted of a long white gown with wings sprouting from the back and a halo on my head. The blackout came as scheduled and I rushed onto the stage with the rostrum. Jack, wearing full modern evening dress, came from the other side clutching a chair. I positioned the rostrum, he the chair and, just as I lifted my skirts to get up on the it, the lights came on. There, framed at the back of the stage, was an angel about to climb up on a chair revealing, beneath his seraphic gown, a pair of modern jeans. A middle-aged gentleman in a dress suit was holding the chair for him. This was confusing for the audience because, even in Ireland, people didn't wear dress suits in their legends. However, I leapt up quickly and Jack, rather than leave the stage, stood sideways behind me.

The on-stage 'peasants' had fallen to their knees in baffled adoration, facing me – or rather us. I could see some of the peasants, particularly Eamon Morrissey, shaking with uncontrollable mirth. At this point the tape started and I began miming my heavenly prose. About two-thirds of the way through, with a deafening silence, the tape broke; another disaster on a Very Bad Night. I stood there, jaw slack, and Jack whispered, 'I'll make the speech, Michael. Continue moving your mouth.' I mouthed gibberish, in as controlled a manner as I possibly could, while a thin, disembodied, slightly reedy voice, I thought – certainly in comparison to the heavenly choirs and echoing bass that had gone before – wafted from behind me.

After the performance, at a reception at the Irish Embassy in Paris, Ray McAnally, who before the show had walked out onto the stage in his dressing gown and treated the early members of the audience to his vocal warm-up exercises, complained loudly to Jack McGowran about our ham-fisted endeavours and about Jack's and everybody else's carelessness in losing the set. Jack was somewhat miffed. Later at the same function, Jack returned to Ray, grinning widely as he pointed out the credits on the programme for the night, where the director was named as one, Ray McAnally! Ray was not amused.

I often wondered what Beckett thought of it all. Perhaps he was there on the second night, when things improved marginally. One thing is for certain – the following day the Parisian newspapers made Celtic mincemeat of us!

Small Screen Looms Large

A great new enterprise was about to be launched in the Emerald Isle. We were to get our very own television station. 'Telefís Éireann' it was to be called and advertisements were placed in all the national newspapers offering employment to studio trainees. Everybody applied. This was the great new frontier.

I applied and was called for interview in a big building down on Clarendon Street. I told of my vast experience in the theatre and in radio and so on and, in time, I received a letter offering me a job, one of only twelve jobs, as studio trainee. I thought about it for about a day and decided there was nothing I could think of that could be more boring in life, with the possible exception of the office at Castrol, than twiddling around with knobs and buttons and wearing headphones and trying to learn how things worked – and not being able to fix them if they didn't. So I wrote back immediately and said thanks, but no thanks. Among the chosen twelve were the late Barry Kelly; ace cameraman Tony Barry, who went on to become one of our best producers; floor manager Charlie Roberts; and my boss at Radio Publicity, Adrian Cronin.

What would have happened to me had I accepted that job? Would I now be comfortably ensconced in the higher echelons of RTE, embroiled in the internecine politics of the station, creating new ways of avoiding meeting my staff and inventing ploys to keep the independent sector at bay? Certainly, my family and most of my friends at the time thought I was mad to turn down the job.

Nonetheless, I did feature on the opening night of Telefís Éireann, on 31 December 1960. Eamon Morrissey and myself had been up the mountains that day, as was our wont (we both liked the countryside), and afterwards we met up with our mutual pal, Tish Barry, who is now an independent producer. We decided we would disport ourselves down near the Gresham, where festivities were promised and where the new station was to be officially opened.

It was snowing when we arrived and waited outside for something to happen. There was dancing and general horseplay and, eventually, a singer (Patrick O'Hagan, we found out later) came out and began to sing Irish songs on a platform outside the Gresham. We thought this was hilarious, and we thought it would be even more hilarious if we joined in with the rest of the crowd and pelted him with snowballs. This we did with gusto. I wasn't to know that the high spirits of the crowd were being immortalised by the eagle-eyed studio trainees of the infant service and that my mother, who was sitting at home, would recognise her dearly beloved horsing around in the snow in the centre of the city with, as she put it later, 'all the other gurriers of the area'. Some of the coverage is still in the archives and I gather I'm quite visible in one or two sections.

By a curious coincidence, Eileen also appeared on the television on the opening night. RTE recorded a series of shots of 'typical Irish beauties' for the occasion and Eileen was well to the fore, acquiring instant fame herself.

* * *

At home, Declan had decided to break the family mould. Having completed his Leaving Certificate at Synge Street, extremely successfully as it turned out, he came home to my mother one Friday lunchtime in early July and told her that he was heading off the next day, Saturday, for a week or so. An order of priests, the Legionaries of Christ, had visited the school and had invited some volunteers for a few weeks' holiday in their house at Bundoran in County Donegal.

My mother was caught in a dilemma. She expected Declan to go into University College Dublin in September, where he was going to study engineering. On the other hand, here was the call of religion on her own doorstep. As I have mentioned, she was a deeply religious woman who went to mass in Rathgar Church every morning and devotions in the evening, and, although she had given up on the family rosary due to lack of interest all round, she did counsel all of us on a regular basis to pray to the likes of St Anthony and, in my case, St Jude.

Anyway, Declan said he'd only be gone for a few weeks and then he'd be home again. So all was agreed, and by lunchtime the next day he was gone. He was seventeen years of age at the time. He didn't see his family, nor they him, for the next nine years. Apart from me, that is, because during the following week he telephoned me from Bundoran and invited me to come up and join him for a few days. He had told the order about his older brother and they insisted that he issue the invitation on their behalf. I hitched my way up, wearing jeans and the little red bomber jacket which I thought made me look like James Dean in *Rebel Without a Cause*. (In fact, I kept that jacket for about ten years.)

I arrived at the house in Bundoran on the back of a motorbike and was just in time for supper. Declan greeted me and we went in to a large dining-room, where about thirty boys and various clerical figures were mingling. The oldest priest gave instructions in Spanish for us to take our seats (I knew this because everybody moved to their seats after he had spoken!) He indicated that I should sit on his right-hand side, while Declan sat opposite. We didn't actually sit, however, we stood, and there was a very long silence. I looked up and caught Declan's eye across the table. He nodded at me, and suddenly the actor in me emerged. I immediately felt guilty that I had missed my cue. I assumed that Declan's look was to tell me that the next move was mine, so I proceeded to recite aloud the grace before meals.

I sensed a general tremor of excitement as I started to speak – but not for long. I couldn't remember beyond the first line, after which I paused, blinking helplessly at Declan. One of the clerical figures came to my rescue and completed the prayer and we all sat down. It transpired that there were no verbal offerings of thanksgiving, that this was done in silence, and that I had created a rather unusual precedent – particularly in getting it wrong.

I stayed three days in all and it wasn't a success. Declan and I became involved in a brotherly brawl while playing basketball and I found generally that the restrictions, charmingly applied though they were, were unacceptable to my innate sense of individuality. We had to move in a group all the time – swim together, walk together, play together – not chat to the locals, and generally live the life of a community. So I returned to Dublin, not realising that it would be many years before I would see my beloved brother again.

In September, my mother received a letter from Declan informing her that he was now in Spain, in Salamanca, and he was going to try out the priesthood to see if it suited him. She was overjoyed. She had, by now, visited the Legion's headquarters in Leopardstown in County Dublin, just beside the racecourse, and had been treated like a visiting dignitary. She was incredibly impressed by the cleanliness of the students, by their charm, their good manners and the depth of their religious commitment. The Legion was to become a focal point in her life.

During the following couple of years, I had occasion to meet with the founder and head of the order, Father Maciel, who seemed quite taken with the prospect that I might consider joining. Where he got this idea from I don't know, because I had no interest from the very beginning. A brilliant man, then in his late fifties, he had founded the order in his native Mexico and created a hugely successful, if right-wing, force in his own country, that had now expanded impressively into Europe. He asked me to join, even going so far as to offer me a lay job in his order's university in Mexico city where I could teach English. I declined with thanks.

Anyway, the Legion entered my family's life and we theirs. Within a couple of years, Catherine had decided that she, too, would like to experience life in the Legion, and so she became a lay missionary for them. This entailed moving, lock, stock, and barrel, into a house that the Legion was renting in the leafy suburb of Foxrock. Her function, and that of the other girls in the house, was to enter UCD and infiltrate the student ranks, enticing as many of them as possible to attend their house of prayer. She was not encouraged to have any communication with her family, except on Sundays when a two-hour visiting period was permitted.

My mother was in clover. Not alone was she now guaranteed a place of honour in this life as the 'mother of all religion', but she was also guaranteed at least a very good seat in the next life. Declan was continuing his studies in Salamanca and we received glowing reports of his progress. I remember there was even serious talk in our family of Declan becoming the first ever Irish Pope – and 'Pope Declan' did have a pretty impressive ring to it!

The icing on the cake was when John decided that he, too, would like to sample spiritual certainty and become a Legionary. Off he went to Spain, despite my protestations.

Neither my sister Pat nor I were as impressed as everyone else with the Legion. I found them too good to be true and I thought their philosophy was altogether too right-wing – bordering on Fascism. They based their aspirations, as far as I could see, on converting and consorting with the rich and, to that end, they taught their young men and women how to disport themselves in a genteel, sophisticated way, what wines to choose, how to sit, what books to read and, in general, how to become a confidante of the well-to-do. And it seemed to work. The upper classes in Mexico and Spain had certainly succumbed to the blandishments of the Legion, and the Legion was benefiting in no uncertain terms. New houses were being established throughout Europe, and now the USA. Even my father was beginning to believe in the possibility of having to attend the installation of the first Irish Pope. As long as he didn't have to make a speech, I think it was fine by him.

I kept in touch, as best I could, with John. I had told him I thought the whole thing was 'for the birds' and, if he needed me to help him get away, just to make one phone call and I'd be there – wherever it was.

We had discovered that Declan had been involved in a major car crash in Spain and had received quite serious injuries, but we were not told until afterwards when he was well on the way to recovery.

Catherine's situation was ludicrous. If she saw any of her family in the street, she was instructed not to speak to, or acknowledge them. I considered all this utter nonsense and wasn't behind the door about saying so.

Ma, of course, was now a maternal icon for the Legionaries; she was actually known as 'Ma'. When she visited the college every Sunday and Thursday, she was fêted by young men with slicked down hair wearing exquisite black soutanes. Father Maciel himself even called her 'Ma'. She adored it all. She looked at Pat and myself and, I'm sure, wondered where had she got these two hard-edged cynics who refused to get carried along on the wave of religious euphoria. I used to wonder aloud how Vernon Grove would look when they built the cathedral where number six now stood and where the three Murphy saints were born. She didn't enjoy that kind of irreverent humour.

About a year later, after John had returned from Salamanca and was ensconced – all brushed up and well-washed – in the college at Leopardstown, I received a phone call. It was John, low-key as ever.

'Michael,' he said urgently into the telephone, 'Could you collect me? I want to get out.'

'Be standing at the hall door in half an hour and I'll be there,' I said. And that's how he left. He literally bolted, without even taking a bag.

I had a jacket for him, which he donned as soon as he had divested himself of his soutane, and I took him straight to Lamb Doyle's pub, where he enjoyed a nice creamy pint of Guinness and a sharp hard Jameson.

Catherine stayed in her vocation for another six months or so, but her leaving took a different form. While in Foxrock, she met and fell in love with one of the novitiates who was based in Leopardstown, a handsome young Spaniard called José Marie Huerta. How they ever managed to get together I'll never know, but a handsome couple they made. She, a dashing high-spirited redhead, and he, a swarthy handsome Spaniard. José's vocation had not been going too well either. Deeply religious though he was, he didn't seem to fit in at all well with the mores of the Legion of Christ, and so he either left, or was asked to leave, I don't know which. Catherine also left and, within a matter of a year or two, wedding bells followed. They lived first in Mexico and then in Spain, and my sister gave birth to four lovely children. Unfortunately, the marriage was not a happy one and they broke up just a couple of years ago.

John, in the meantime, made a name for himself at the time of their wedding by becoming altogether too familiar with one of the beautiful Spanish in-laws on the eve of the big occasion and, even worse, getting caught.

Declan moved to Rome and thence to Mexico, where he became the right-hand confidante of the founder. He was, it seemed, destined for great things. His ordination was delayed for over a year, however. We never heard the full story, but apparently he had become embroiled in a 'spot of bother' in Mexico. While he was preaching somewhere, one of the local community, many of whom were anti-Church, attacked him with a hoe or a shovel or some such thing. Declan, who is a fine big fellow – about six-foot-three – smartly punched the man and broke his jaw. This was not what was expected of a spokesman for the Lord. Declan was apparently forced to work to support this man's family for the course of the next year and his ordination was delayed.

We were to know none of this until we all finally met Declan the day before his ordination in Rome. I was married at this stage, but could not afford to bring Eileen with me, so I went alone for the two days. Ma was having one of her bad spells and was wheeled to the plane in Dublin airport in a wheelchair. However, as we were flying on a crisp clear day over middle Europe, somebody murmured, 'There's the Alps,' and lo and behold, the patient leapt to her feet and, brushing aside other passengers and sundry members of her own family, glued her nose to the porthole and gave thanks to the Lord for his magnitude. The family referred to it afterwards as 'the miracle of the Alps'. From then on she was like a two-year-old.

It was my father, whose leg was giving him trouble, who became the laggard and for whom we had to wait as we wandered the streets of the Vatican. We met Declan and there was a wonderful reunion. He looked healthy and hadn't changed much. That night, I took Pat and Catherine on a pub crawl and the next morning we were, all three of us, dying of hangovers.

I had been invited to read the lesson at the ordination, which was a group ordination. All the families of the Legion were gathered in the same convent as ourselves and we had to take a bus to the Vatican for the ceremony. The bus was forced to wait for me, as I was feeling quite ill.

When my mother, who was somewhat exasperated by my behaviour, saw me coming, she said loudly to everyone on the bus, 'God, would you look at him! You'd think he was walking on eggshells.'

In photographs of the occasion, my face looked a curious shade of green and apparently I could hardly be heard as I read the lesson. Many of the people present didn't know whether I was speaking Latin, Spanish, or English. But it was a joyous occasion, nonetheless.

Bless me, Father, I'm Lying!

I was now immersed in sponsored programmes, with a little bit of acting thrown in for good measure. I was writing and producing all of Radio Publicity's programmes, such as Rank's with Sheila Cunningham, Willwood with Bonnie O'Reilly, Lemon's with Vincent Dowling, Colgate–Palmolive, and so on. It was Colgate–Palmolive, in fact, who were instrumental in my first ever 'live' broadcast. Frank Purcell was ill and didn't turn up one day, so I was obliged to present the programme live from the old studio in Henry Street. It was a terrifying fifteen minutes for me, but it went off without any major incident.

The sponsored programmes were the most popular programmes of their time. They ran from eight until nine in the morning, and from one o'clock until three during the afternoon. In those days, Radio Éireann used to close down between ten in the morning and a quarter to one, and between three and five in the afternoon. The big sponsored programmes of the time were the Philip's show with Denis Brennan, the Donnelly's Sausages programme with Niall Boden, Cecil Barror did the Bird's Jelly Deluxe programme, Frank Kelly the Glen Abbey show, and Harry Thuillier effectively did all the rest.

Harry was a phenomenon of the time. How he had managed to corner the market in sponsored programmes, I do not know, but he was the most prolific producer and presenter of his time. He had a swashbuckling, carefree air about him and was very entertaining in company. He took the whole thing, it appeared, with a grain of salt, and laughed that people would pay him to do something he found so easy. And he seemed to be making incredible money.

One day he phoned me and asked me if I would stand in for him on, I think, the Stork Margarine programme and I said I would.

'I'm not going to be able to pay you much money, Marshal,' he said (he called everyone either 'Marshal' or 'Sunshine'), 'But I'll give you half of my own fee. Is that okay?'

'Not at all Harry – I'll do it for nothing,' I said.

'No, no. I'll give you half my own fee,' he said.

At that time the fees that I was receiving, and indeed paying, were no more than three to five guineas a time. Guineas, never pounds.

'The most I can manage is ten guineas for the programme,' Harry told me.

I was stunned. Ten guineas for one programme – and that was only half his fee? The calculations made my head spin. Was he telling me the truth? I don't know. Harry was of a gambling nature and enjoyed setting people up. I recall he and Jimmy McGee, who worked with Harry on a number of programmes, betting one day on the speed of raindrops running down a windowpane. The betting was fairly significant too, ten to twenty pounds a throw, which was quite a lot of money in those days.

Harry's many *faux pas* on air became legendary and were recounted often – and with great affection, I might add. He both presented and produced the Tayto family quiz, for which Jimmy wrote the questions. Harry was never one to do much homework and was well capable of flying by the seat of his pants, but this very often led to significant errors in the programme. On one occasion, he asked a ten-year-old boy a question.

contd on p. 81

My mother's family. She is standing second from the left. Auntie May is standing on the right.

My mother and father shortly after their own wedding at my father's sister Joan's marriage to Pat Kerins. To me, it speaks volumes. My father is on the extreme left, while my mother is centre stage, behind the groom, in the fur coat. Da's mother, that formidable character, is wearing the black sombrero.

Taking care of little brother, Declan.

First Holy Communion. A paragon of good,
Catholic, Irish youth-hood!

This was on the front page of *The Irish Times* in 1953.
Left to right: John Kelly, Declan my brother, Tim Healy and myself.

EXAMINATION SUCCESSES

THIRD YEAR

5th Row : A. Searson, J. Woulfe, L. Hollingsworth, T. Anderson, P. McCowen, H. Wilson.
4th Row : I. Sexton, J. Richardson, N. McGrath, P. Flynn, R. McCreery, J. Ryan, K. Moore, G. Begley, B. Cowley, E. Power, N. Kelly.
3rd Row : P. Kiernan, F. O'Kelly, J. Garry, R. Ekins, T. Healy, C. Carr, D. Blake, J. Mercer, R. Byrne, E. Kelly, B. McKenna, S. Tormey.
2nd Row : C. Bruton, T. Bermingham, D. Henry, L. Fahy, M. Murphy, B. Wilcox, J. Cotter, G. Duffy, P. Williams, I. Hynes, E. Treacy, V. Morris, M. Power.
1st Row : A. Saunders, P. McKay, C. O'Brien, G. Morrissey, Rev. E. J. O'Sharkey, O.Carm.; Mr. T. Fitzsimons, Rev. W. J. Ardiff, O.Carm.; Rev. J. D. McCouaig, O.Carm.; P. Fitzmaurice, J. C. Kelly, J. J. Kelly, M. MacMahon.

The heading 'Examination Successes' is one of the greatest misnomers ever. The following year we did our Intermediate Certificate and managed to attain Terenure's worst results ever — over 50% failure. I was one of those 50%.

Left to right: (back) Myself, Patricia, Ma and Da; (front) John and Catherine.

Ma and Da.

1954. *Left to right:* (back) Myself, Patricia and Declan; (front) John and Catherine.

The young a.. ., aged 18, demonstrating his sincerity, reliability, versatility, expressiveness — and his new watch, a present from his mother!

1963. Eileen and myself on our first formal date, a dress dance in the Shelbourne Rooms. I had an old 'banger' of a Volkswagen Beetle and as I was driving her home, the passenger seat literally broke in half. Eileen's mother was totally opposed to her going out with 'one of those actor-types'.

1965. The wedding day. Fr. Yepez, who couldn't speak or read English had married us — or so we chose to believe!

The wedding reception at the Royal Marine Hotel, Dun Laoghaire.
Left to right: My cousin Paul Deering, Tony Dwyer, myself and Eileen,
Maureen Field and my sister Catherine.

My mother on our wedding day with
one of the priests from the Legion of
Christ, Fr. Cointreau.

Ma with her three tickets to heaven.
Left to right: John, Catherine and
Declan.

Eileen's mother, Gran, and myself enjoying each other's company (and we did) in Butlins.

Ma and Da with their first grandchild, Elaine.

St. Stephen's Day, 1981. Da, in my house with Mark, two days before he died.

'What is the name of the church dignitary who is the president of an island in the Mediterranean?'

The child thought awhile and answered, correctly, 'Archbishop Makarios.' There was a telling pause as Harry scrutinised the answer in front of him.

'No,' he said. 'I'm sorry, we can't give you that. The answer is of course Archbishop "Macka-rye-us".'

He also presented a live programme in the mornings for a clock company, during which he was encouraged to give as many 'time checks' as possible, to verify the accuracy of the clocks he was advertising. The problem was that the time checks were all minutes 'to' the hour, and Harry found this extremely difficult since his talent was more inclined towards addition than subtraction. So he would give the time, then immediately correct it, then go back to his earlier guess and find that he had misquoted the hour. The programme was scheduled to run for a year, but I believe it was taken off after thirteen weeks. It was understandable that time checks of the order of 'The time now, by my so-and-so watch, is thirteen minutes to – sorry, eleven minutes to – no, that should be six minutes to eight – sorry, nine' would be unacceptable to any self-respecting time keeper.

Harry also presented the Jacob's *Come Fly With Me* programme, in which he would take an Aer Lingus flight to what were then exotic locations, like Rome or Brussels or Copenhagen. He would interview some passengers on the flight and then describe the joys of his destination when he got there. Because Harry's schedule was so hectic, he often missed a flight or took the wrong one. I recall him recording a live commentary on a bullfight in Lower Mount Street; the presence of local Spanish enthusiasts was later dubbed in from a sound-effects record. Harry had missed the flight to Barcelona and had promised the client a commentary on a bullfight for that week. Places and people confused him sometimes, too. On one flight he asked two gentlemen where they were from.

'Manchester,' they answered, and Harry observed 'So, you're Manchurians.'

But I gather his last flight came when he created a bit of an incident on a plane. Instead of heading for Brussels, Harry found himself flying to Copenhagen by mistake. The problem was that the sponsor and the listeners were expecting him to go to Brussels. During the flight, he spoke to two elderly passengers who had, unlike Harry, limited English. He explained his dilemma to them in pidgin English and told them that, when he spoke to them on tape, they were to pretend they were going to Brussels and not to Copenhagen. They nodded their assent and seemed to understand, so Harry commenced the interview.

'So,' he said, 'You're heading all the way to Brussels?'

'No,' they answered. 'We're going to Copenhagen.'

'No,' Harry replied. 'Brussels. We're going to Brussels.'

'We are not,' the hapless passengers replied. 'We are going to Copenhagen.'

'No,' Harry said. 'Remember, this plane goes to Brussels.'

'No, Copenhagen.'

'Brussels,' said Harry. 'You agreed.'

'No. We want to go to Copenhagen.'

'Well, Brussels is where we're going,' said Harry.

At this point, the woman passenger, who was extremely distressed, stood up and started screaming for the air hostess. The man turned on Harry and commenced shouting at him in his own language, while Harry attempted to switch off his tape recorder. Meanwhile, some of the other passengers, many of whom had heard the conversation, had passed the word that they were all on the wrong aircraft and were calling for the captain. That, I heard, was Harry's last radio flight.

It was Jimmy McGee who gave me my first break in radio. Stewart's Cash Prices, a supermarket chain, had decided, at Jimmy's urging, to present two half-hour programmes per week, from eleven o'clock until eleven-thirty at night. Jimmy invited Noel McCall, another embryonic presenter, and myself to present the two nights. The programmes entailed interviewing showband stars, playing music from the charts and new Irish records, and generally making pleasant sounds. The programmes proved to be very successful.

I was also doing a little bit of acting on television. I was given a part in a series called *Down at Flannery's*, where I played the juvenile lead and had a passionate on-screen relationship with Lelia Doolin, now head of the Irish Film Board. I was also cast in a Jim Fitzgerald production of a TV play about a bunch of young IRA men heading North to plant a bomb. There was no mention of political correctness in those days! There was another play, *All the King's Horses*, which starred Martin Dempsey and Hal Roach.

However, I was gradually moving away from the theatre. Although I enjoyed the process of acting and the bohemian life, there was no possibility of earning a decent living. And Eileen and I were about to be married.

So it was that I applied for the job of announcer with Radio Éireann and, by the skin of my teeth – and other people's – I got on the announcers' course. The other aspiring announcers on my course included Maurice O'Doherty, Lorna Madigan, Padraig Dolan and Tony Lyons. Maurice went on to become one of RTE's best ever newsreaders, Lorna is currently Head of Radio Presentation, Padraig became a very successful radio producer and presenter and Tony Lyons was RTE's public relations officer for many years.

Tony was the first of us to get any employment at all. He was head-hunted by the newsroom and invited to read the late-night news on radio. Tony, an engaging, outgoing fellow, was only too happy to oblige and he was the envy of us all. He had a habit then, and ever after, of wearing sunglasses. I used to say he wore them because he didn't want people recognising him from the late night radio news and crowding him for autographs, but I was just being bitchy. Tony, in fact, unwittingly featured in another blush-inducing episode of my life.

I was living in Rathgar, as I have mentioned, and I felt the need to go to confession. The sin I had committed was so grave that I decided to betake myself to the next parish, Rathmines, to obtain forgiveness.

Rathmines was Tony's parish, but that, needless to say, didn't occur to me at the time. I went to confession, confessed the gravity of my transgressions, recited the act of contrition and was about to take my leave when the priest said, 'Pardon me, just before you go. . .'

'Yes, Father?' I said.

'Do you mind if I ask you a personal question?'

'Eh . . . no, Father,' I mumbled.

'Do I recognise the voice?' he asked. My stomach sank. I thought maybe he had heard me on the Stewart's Cash Prices Show.

'I'm not sure, Father,' I said slowly.

'That wouldn't be Tony Lyons, the newsreader?' he asked.

'It would, Father,' came the prompt reply.

'Delighted to meet you,' said the priest.

'Me too, Father.'

'God bless.'

'God bless you too, Father.'

I left the confessional in a flurry of confusion and shame. I was appalled at what I had done. I had *lied in confession*. There was nothing else for me to do but cross the church to another confession box and confess my more recent sin. I never told Tony that story, but I often wondered if he was subjected to any askew glances from one of the priests of his parish.

At the end of the six-week course, five of the seven participants were accepted as part-time announcers. I wasn't, I regret to say, one of the chosen five, but again Denis Meehan came to my rescue. He asked me if I would promise to continue my Irish studies in my own time over the next year or so. I swore I would.

'Right,' he said. 'We'll take you on and hope for the best.'

And so it was that I came to join the élite of Terry Wogan, Andy O'Mahony, David Timlin, Una Sheehy, John Skehan, Brigid Kilfeather, Liam Devally – the big names of the time.

The Happiest Day of your Life?

As the day of the wedding, 15 September 1965, approached, tensions were running high. My mother did not approve of my marrying Eileen (of my marrying at all, if the truth were known) and had made her feelings very clear in a myriad of small ways.

Matters came to a head about a month before the wedding. My mother sat me down 'to have a few words' with me. She told me that, one, I was too young to get married at twenty-three years of age; secondly, I didn't have a proper job; and, thirdly, in her opinion, Eileen and her family were socially inferior to ourselves. She asked me if I knew that Eileen's uncle, who kept pigs, drove a 'slop wagon'. I told her I did know and that it made not the slightest bit of difference to me. I also told her that, if she felt that that would be a problem with regard to the guest list on the big day, she needn't worry. Apparently Eileen's mother, who was quite elderly and widowed, didn't get on too well with some members of her family and so only a few of them would be present.

This didn't stop my mother from continuing to say unpleasant and hurtful things about the likely consequences of the marriage in the future. I was still very much in thrall to my mother and knew that her biggest problem was that I would be leaving home – and for another woman. But I was angry and hurt. While she was in full spate, I stood up, stepped back from the chair, pointed at her and told her to 'fuck off' and 'mind her own business'. That was undoubtedly the cathartic moment of our relationship. It was never the same afterwards. She neither forgot nor forgave my outburst.

On Eileen's side, her mother had, for some reason that I was never aware of, run foul of her own family and had decided to invite only a handful of them to the wedding. This resulted in a number of anonymous phone calls to me and to Eileen at the office and at home. Eileen was told that, on her wedding day, people would be waiting outside the church with buckets of mud to throw over her as she emerged from the church. She was very frightened and, despite all the reassurances I could muster, was extremely nervous on the day.

We were married in Rathfarnham Church and my best man was Tony Dwyer, with whom I had been friends since our Brendan Smith Academy days. Eileen's bridesmaid was her friend Maureen Field. The mass was celebrated by Father Yepez who was, of course, a member of the Legion of Christ (a concession to the family) and who spoke almost no English. We often pondered in later years whether we were truly married at all, as Father Yepez had never officiated at a marriage in his life before. Nobody understood what he was saying and nobody was sure where he would move to next on the altar. The poor man was killed a few years later in a motor crash.

Declan was not permitted to be present, as he was still safely in the clutches of the Legion in some far distant land. John served the mass. The breakfast took place in the Royal Marine Hotel, Dun Laoghaire, and was pervaded by a sense of relief that nothing untoward had happened after the ceremony. There were, of course, speeches. A married friend of my father's, who was quite famously conducting a long-term affair with his guest at the wedding, made a very moving speech about the sanctity of marriage. Vincent Dowling, representing the world of theatre, said some kind words about nobody saying unkind words about me. Jimmy McGee spoke wittily about knowing Eileen for many years as receptionist in Eamonn Andrews' studios and wondering how she had come to such a sticky end, with a such disreputable character as myself.

Both Eileen and I thought the day would never end. There was a photograph taken at the airport as we were leaving on our honeymoon. I have Eileen by the hand, my face looks drawn and anxious, she's turning back to wave and I look as if I'm saying to her, 'Come on, let's get the hell out of here, fast!' Those certainly were my sentiments, and hers as well.

When we returned from our honeymoon, which we spent in the mountain village of Igls in Austria, it was to find that my mother, who had been somewhat remote at the wedding, now wouldn't speak to me at all. It took me a number of days to find out why. It transpired that Eileen's mother, whom I always called Gran, had been injudicious enough, on the day of the wedding, to tell my mother how lucky she was being married to such a fine man as my father. This was precisely the one sentence not to use on such an auspicious day and Gran really should have known better. She had spent the previous Christmas Day in our family house in Vernon Grove and such was the atmosphere that, when she returned home, she was physically ill. She had never before experienced tension like it. Eileen, who had in the early stages found it quite incredible that a family could live in such a high state of nervous tension, had become slightly inured, but was still shocked to find her mother, who enjoyed good health, stricken after the experience.

I told my mother she was being ridiculous and that she should make allowances for someone as old as Gran, who was unaware of the situation at home and who simply meant to be kind and complimentary. But Ma was having none of it.

Matters worsened the first Christmas after Eileen and I had moved in to a one-room apartment in Dundrum village while waiting for our new house, a three-bedroomed semi on the new Ludford Road estate in Ballinteer, to be completed. I was still only a part-time announcer and was quite impoverished. I bought my mother a large dress bracelet for Christmas, thinking she would like it. On St Stephen's Day, I received a phone call from her asking me to come down to the house that evening, as she wished to speak to me.

She was sitting at the table in the dining room with Pat, Catherine and John in attendance. She told me how insulted she was at the crassness and thoughtlessness of my Christmas present and wondered how I could humiliate her so. I was twenty-four years of age by now, but I was distraught. I begged her forgiveness. I went down on my knees in front of her and sobbed. My sister Pat told me many years later that she would never forget the sight of her big brother, who always appeared so sure of himself and so resilient, being berated and humiliated like a child at his mother's knee.

I made my mother promise me that she would come into the city the next day and I would buy her a 'proper Christmas present'. So, the next day, the two of us went into town and I spent what little money I had left on an alarm clock-cum-coffee-maker, which pleased her no end. Eileen was angry at my mother and even more angry at me for allowing myself to be bullied into spending money we plainly didn't have to spare.

My father simply reversed out of my life at this stage. He offered no advice in terms of buying the house or getting a mortgage, even though he had bought and sold so many houses himself. Maybe he thought I would have rejected his advice out of hand, I don't know.

My mother ensured that I now became the 'bad guy' in the family and she used every opportunity to make my brothers and sisters aware of her feelings. When my sister Pat met and fell in love with her future husband, Fenton McCarthy, Ma wrote to Declan that Fenton had become 'the son that Michael never was'. Declan told me about this soon afterwards in a letter and I was desperately hurt. Then my mother, who sometimes visited us in her peremptory manner in our little house in Ludford Road, turned against Fenton for some reason. One evening in our house, she told me how Pat and Fenton had been abusing her and her hospitality, how they had been inconsiderate towards her, and so on. I drove her to Vernon Grove and, by the time we got there, I was, as in the past, well and truly wound up and ready to go into battle. She had metaphorically pointed me and fired. I went into the house and attacked Pat for her and Fenton's alleged behaviour and told her to tell Fenton that if he didn't change his ways he'd have me to reckon with. Pat was, naturally, desperately hurt that I would turn against her and it created a major rift in our relationship. It was, in fact, my mother's imagination – or call it what you will – manipulating her loved ones as usual. I was foolish, needless to say, in not being able to see through it by now, but I had had many years of conditioning, and it was hard for me to confront the reality of her behaviour.

Eileen gave birth to Elaine, the first of our four beautiful children, in January 1967 and, to our surprise, we followed with our second daughter, Carol, in December of that year. I remember Eileen coming home from Mount Carmel, carrying Carol in her arms. Elaine crawled out to the front door to meet her and Eileen burst into tears. Two children in one year was a terrible responsibility for a young woman. Eileen by now was no longer working; it was not acceptable then for a married woman to go out to work. I certainly didn't want her to and she was not inclined to, either. It is extraordinary how attitudes changed over the next few years.

Those times were not easy. We had no money. We could only furnish two rooms, a bedroom upstairs and the dining-room downstairs. One hilarious evening, we entertained some of my radio colleagues. Denis and Sylvia Meehan, Terry and Helen Wogan, John and Winnie Skehan, Maurice and Phyl O'Doherty, as well as Eileen and I, were forced to squeeze ourselves into the partly-furnished dining-room for the evening. Maurice had cooked the meal, a curry of his own devising, which left us all reeling for days afterwards.

Babysitting was also a problem. Eileen had no brothers or sisters and my sisters, through my mother's intervention, were not inclined to help out with any babysitting duties.

In 1969, I became seriously ill with meningitis and was taken to Clonskeagh Fever Hospital in a coma. I was given nine lumbar punctures before the needle hit the right spot and brought me relief. When my mother arrived, she brushed Eileen aside and, although I was not permitted visitors, she announced: 'It's my son and I'm going in.' She came into my room and sat at my bed for a number of hours until I regained consciousness. Eileen, in the meantime, was not allowed to enter the room. That was to be the pattern throughout my illness. Ma, with or without Pat, would sit Eileen out during visiting times, so that Eileen was rarely left alone with me. Also, no one would volunteer to mind Elaine and Carol for her while Eileen came to visit. I certainly don't blame either Pat or Catherine for any of this, as I know that they were conditioned into not offering any help. But, from the point of view of my own family, they were very difficult years.

Into the Breach, Dear Wogan

My broadcasting career was beginning to take off. I had survived the announcer's course, I had managed to scrape in as a part-time announcer and I was now presenting Hospitals Requests, Cyprus Requests and Overseas Requests in a roster with all the other announcers. Terry Wogan was Senior Announcer and we had enjoyed each other's company hugely. He indoctrinated me into the 'joys' of announcing in no uncertain manner!

I was to make my big début announcement, a symphony concert of music by Shostakovich, which I was to announce live from the tiny 'continuity' studio. I was terrified. Terry sat in the big leather armchair in the corner of the studio to – metaphorically – hold my hand, in case I had a nervous breakdown, or died, or cried, or whatever! Came the big moment, I switched on the microphone and launched into my carefully enunciated description of the early life of Shostakovich, articulating every word, rounding vowels and sharpening consonants. It seemed to be going pretty well and I was about halfway down the page when I noticed, out of the corner of my eye, Mr Wogan raising his well-padded figure from the chair and wandering behind me. I sensed, rather than saw, him pour a glass of water, and was aware that he had moved directly behind my back. I was still reading, sounding very much like the good boy in the class, when I felt the back of my collar being pulled away from my neck. I carried on manfully. It was only when I felt the trickle of water being poured down my back that I had the presence of mind to finish whatever sentence I was reading, turn off the microphone, turn around, tell him where to go in a very un-Radio Éireann-like manner and wait till he returned to his chair. I then clicked on the microphone button and continued on my sonorous way. When I had finished, I rounded on him in a mixture of anger and mirth.

'Okay, Murph, you'll do fine,' he said. I had survived the old 'water treatment' with flying colours.

At that time, the senior announcers used to give the junior announcers 'refresher courses'. This entailed working one-to-one for a full day every week. This took various forms. In Brigid Kilfeather's case, you would meet Brigid at ten o'clock in the morning, she would sit you down, run you through a few mispronouncements she had heard you make during the week, test your Irish (which gradually faded out as far as I was concerned, both the test and what little Irish I had garnered), and then we would head off around the auction rooms, where Bridget would pick up some attractive little knick-knacks for her flat.

With Denis Meehan, John Skehan and Terry Wogan, it was different. Denis would ask you, were you interested in losing a pound or two, and would invite you to treat him to a game of golf. Terry would simply say, 'I'll meet you on the first tee at Edmundston at ten o'clock.'

Before teeing off, he would ask me, 'How are things going in the announcing business?'

I'd say, 'Fine, thanks,' and he'd say, 'Right, I'll play you for a pound.'

So, all in all, it was an extremely pleasant way of life, not troubled by too much tension or inconvenience.

I became particularly friendly with John Skehan, whose laconic, laid-back humour really appealed to me. He and I remained friends until his sad death a couple of years ago. We shared a sense of humour and irreverent attitude, and I derived much enjoyment from John's anecdotes and wonderful use of language. John had style. When he was delegated to take someone on a refresher course, John would say, 'If you have any problems, give me a buzz, but not after midday. I'll be at the races in Leopardstown for the afternoon.'

John loved to tell anecdotes about his broadcasting career. He would recall when RTE television first began and he was one of the presenters on the teatime news programme called *Broadsheet*. He was also reading news on radio at the time. He had to read the 6.30 news on radio, then rush down the corridor and into the TV studio where he would go straight into his interview for *Broadsheet*. On one particular occasion, he finished the news, ran down the corridor, was 'miked-up', had time only to utter a casual 'Hello and welcome' to his guest who was sitting in the opposite chair, when they were on air.

'Good evening,' said John. 'I would like to introduce our special guest. He is one of Britain's best-known ornithologists, Mr Trevor Newcombe. You're welcome, Mr Newcombe.'

The gentleman opposite said, 'Sorry, I'm not Trevor Newcombe and I'm not an ornithologist.'

John asked, 'What are you then?'

'A nuclear scientist.'

At this stage of the story, of course, someone – usually me – always said, 'God, what did you talk to him about then, John?'

And John would reply, 'Nuclear science, of course. What else?'

On another occasion, he ran into the studio to find that his guest had not been properly miked-up. Microphones, then, were fairly clumsy affairs that were literally looped like a rope around one's neck and connected to the outside control room. Charlie Roberts, who was floor manager, looped the microphone around the guest's neck just as they were going on air. John made a short, formal introduction, welcoming his guest, at the same time as Charlie, taking a few steps back, caught his foot in the microphone cable. As the camera came onto the guest, he was seen to disappear, with a strangulated cry, head-over-heels over the back of the chair.

Charlie Roberts, himself, was the subject of an oft-repeated story in RTE. He had decided to invest in racing pigeons as a source of extra income and had splashed out £100 on a particularly speedy thoroughbred. When the day of the race came, Charlie instructed his wife, the singer Ann O'Dwyer, that the neighbours were not to hang out their washing, nor indeed was she, that he was to be served all his meals in the garden and that no fires were to be lit. All this so that the returning hero, who was being released in Calais or some such place, would find no distractions or discouragements as he came in to land. He sat in the garden for most of the day and, suddenly, ahead of schedule, he saw the feathered speed merchant circle the house and land on the chimney. The next move was to catch the bird, so that he could retrieve the ring from its leg and stamp the time it had returned upon it. Charlie gleefully began to call the bird down from the chimney. The bird would not move. Charlie cooed, clucked and roared – to no avail. He then went into the house and leaned out of the upstairs bedroom window, clutching onto the drainpipe. The bird still didn't move. Charlie was panic-stricken by this stage. He ran into one of his neighbour's houses and emerged carrying a shotgun. He took aim and fired. It was a perfect shot – the unfortunate bird almost disintegrated. Charlie got the ring, brought it inside, stamped it and waited. The delay had cost him the major prize. The bird, the 'fastest bird in Christendom', had only finished fourth!

The GPO in Henry Street was an extremely agreeable place in which to work, not from an environmental point of view, but purely from a social one. Radio Éireann at that time was home to a number of charming eccentrics, all of whom were inordinately talented in their own way. I recall Roibeard O'Faracháin, the poet, who was Controller of Programmes and who would spend most of a meeting arguing with his staff over whether a word in Irish should have a *sine fada* or not. Francis McManus and Seamus Kavanagh were also larger-than-life characters. But no greater character existed there than my old friend and champion, Denis Meehan.

Denis was talented, gentle and extremely sociable. There was nothing he liked better than to inveigle you into joining him for a bottle of wine and a plate of pasta in some city-centre Italian restaurant after work. There he would regale you with stories and anecdotes. At the end of the evening it was not beyond him to say, 'You don't have a pound, do you?' and you would willingly give it to him, knowing that it might be weeks before you'd see it again.

Denis was thrilled to learn that my father was in the motor business and decided that here was an opportunity to take full advantage of his position as the garage owner's son's boss. He bought an Austin Cambridge from my father. I had recommended his going to my father with some trepidation. Not too long before, I had bought an old banger of a Citroën from him and, when it began to give me major problems, I left it back to him to have it repaired. He kept evading my phone calls and, when I did get him, he avoided answering my questions as to what kind of progress they were making with the car. It transpired, some months later, that he had given it to some 'huckster' down a back lane to fix whatever was wrong with it. However, he couldn't remember which huckster he had given it to and so the car had, quite simply, disappeared! I actually never saw it again.

So, it was with some understandable niggling worry that I had encouraged Denis to buy the car from my father. Sure enough, about six weeks later, Denis came into the continuity studio looking extremely red-faced and flustered. He wanted to know my father's home telephone number. It transpired that, as he was pulling away from the traffic lights at Cornelscourt, he suddenly found his feet were running along the road. The floor of the car had been left behind at the traffic lights! Denis was not amused and nor was I. The situation was ultimately rectified, but not without a few choice exchanges between my father and me.

Maurice O'Doherty, meanwhile, was making tremendous inroads into newsreading. He was possessed of a wonderful baritone voice and tremendous diction. Maurice was another character. He and his wife, Phyl, loved to get all the announcers together in their house for a social evening – saucepans of beef Stroganoff and bring your own wine. There were some hilarious evenings and life-long friendships were forged among the announcers.

Terry was already beginning to move on to greater things. I remember a tape he put together to send over to the BBC which was returned to him because he had wound it the wrong way round. He promptly sent it back, they listened to it and he was immediately offered a job on a BBC night-time radio programme. He was thrilled, and he proceeded to leave these fair shores once a week to commence what eventually was to become his golden career. He was clever about it. I recall him telling me that he was careful how he handled the various producers who could help his cause. He quickly discovered who to invite to what, and his constant joshing and teasing and command of language made him an instant favourite with these often dull BBC types. He knew his strengths, realised that they found his personality attractive, and shamelessly played upon it. We, for our part, were all thrilled for him and were proud to know him and count him as a friend.

In 1971, Terry was to write the sleeve notes for my first (!) LP, as they were called in those days. I enjoyed his tongue-in-cheek approach with a pen. He wrote:

> Everybody has a Mike Murphy in their life. He's the fellow that your mother or sister immediately picked out in the school photograph and said, 'Now, who's that nice-looking boy?' Remember him? 'Course you do – every school has one, tall, handsome, wavy hair and blinding teeth. Even worse, clever with it and good at games as well. All the makings of the most unpopular boy in the school. But that's the worst of the Mike Murphys of this world. You can't dislike them either. Not this Mike Murphy anyway, hard as you may try. The dislike will be overwhelmed by wave after wave of breezy bonhomie, insouciance, joie-de-vivre, and if I could think of another French tag,

I'd let you have that too. Let's just say our boy has charm enough for ten and leave it at that.

Of course, if you've ever spent half-an-hour in Ireland, you'll be familiar with the Murphy features anyway. There, he's always coming out of the wonderful speaking wireless or haunted fishtank at you and in a variety of hats, actor, raconteur, compère, announcer, sports commentator. And those who have heard his impassioned reading of the cattle market report are rarely the same afterwards.

In fact, it was the cattle market report that taught me one of the great lessons of broadcasting. I went over to Madigan's for a few drinks one night, when I was acting station supervisor. The announcer had been taken ill and had had to go home and so I was constrained to read the cattle market report. Unfortunately I had had far too much to drink at the pub and, in the course of trying to decipher the cattle market report, which was bobbing up and down in front of me, I stumbled and stuttered and mumbled so much that eventually I was faded off the air. When I sobered up, I realised what a foolish risk I had taken. Ever after, I was very careful about taking more than one drink before any form of broadcast.

Gay Byrne had been very successful with Granada Television, a success that went almost unnoticed in this country because there was no television culture as yet. Gay had done amazingly well in a very short space of time, and then came back to this country when RTE opened and was the obvious choice when Tom McGrath created the new programme, *The Late Late Show*. I remember, years later, Tom telling me his rationale for *The Late Late Show* and the reason he selected Gay. He wanted to create an impression of an Irish home. The older generation would be represented by the comedian Danny Cummins playing a quick-witted, humorous character. The eldest son would effectively be the host for the evening, and this was where Gay would come in. There would be a sister figure, and here Tom cast a blond woman named Verona Mullen, I think, and then you'd have all sorts of interesting neighbours and guests dropping in for a chat, just as in rural Ireland. These would include such un-rural figures as Denis Franks, Ulick O'Connor, and so on. And so it was that Tom McGrath cast Gay as the 'eldest son' figure – the host of *The Late Late Show*.

The Jimmy McGee All-Stars had also begun and, every Monday night that we could manage, a bunch of us representing the entertainment industry and showbands would head off around the country to play Gaelic football against teams of veteran players. It was exhilarating, it was fun and it raised a huge amount of money for charity.

Jimmy himself took the game very seriously indeed. Although not a spectacularly convincing looking figure on the field, he made up for his lack of pace by the quantity of vocal endeavour he expended. He would invariably play for most of the match and then have himself substituted when he got too tired shouting. I recall an occasion in Shillelagh, County Wicklow, when he left the field (to muted applause, it must be said) and decided to take a short cut back to the pavilion. To do this, he had to climb over a barbed wire fence. Unfortunately, as he climbed up and threw a leg over the top of the fence, he became entangled. He began to bellow like a stuffed pig. He couldn't go forward or back. He was actually impaled astride the barbed wire fence. The match was stopped, the crowd gathered round and, to much witty badinage and high spirits and even genuine concern, a number of members of both teams went to either side of the barbed wire fence and gently – *very* gently – lifted Jimmy bodily off the offending wire.

Showbands were now all the rage. The Top Ten record charts were in full swing. There was even talk of 'payola'. It was rumoured that a certain radio producer was amenable to 'fixing' the Top Ten if the manager of the band left a ten-pound note wrapped in the *Evening Herald* after a drink in Madigan's. But was it true? I really don't know.

During the course of a reception to launch a new record, of which there were hundreds, Joe Linnane retired to the gents to relieve himself. He was standing at the urinal when a showband type sidled up to him, pressed a five-pound note into his breast pocket and said companionably, 'There you are now, Joe. Thanks very much for all the plays and here's to a few more.'

Joe protested and mumbled, asking who he was, but the impresario just held up two hands.

'Have a drink on me and the lads, Joe,' he said. 'And there's more where that came from.'

Technical Trouble at the Dentures

I was presenting Hospitals Requests at this stage and was beginning to gain some popularity. I remember playing a brand new record called 'Gentle Mother' by a singer named Big Tom and making some relatively caustic comment about it. A few days later, I was confronted in the corridor in Radio Éireann (the longest 'jacks' in Europe, as it was quaintly called) by a huge, ambling man with a blond fringe. He walked towards me and I stepped aside to let him pass. But he didn't pass. He looked down at me and said, in a broad Monaghan accent, 'Are you Mike Murphy?'

'I am,' I said.

'Well, I'm Big Tom,' he said.

'Oh, hello. . .' I said, beginning to feel a little edgy.

'I heard what you said about me on the radio the other day,' he said, not unpleasantly.

'Oh, did you?' I hedged.

'I did,' he said, 'And in future,' poking a finger at my chest, 'kindly just play the record and say nothing!' And he was gone.

Brendan Balfe had joined the announcing staff by now and he and

I soon became inseparable. We both enjoyed the other's approach to life and we had a similar sense of humour. We were also pretty impoverished at the time and couldn't always afford to go to the pub for a drink, so we developed what became known as the 'hotel crawl'. We would go into city-centre hotels, look up the list of functions that were taking place in the hotel and then saunter nonchalantly into the reception, looking as though we were invited guests. It always worked. Once we were so desperate for a drink that we joined the Catholic Young Men's Society in O'Connell Street as life members, for five pounds, which we promised we would send on in the morning. I hate to admit it, but I don't think we ever did!

Some years later, Brendan, myself and Larry Gogan became the Presenters' Working Party, representing all the other compères in negotiations, for fees and conditions and so on, with RTE. I acquired the reputation of being somewhat fiery at some of these meetings. Brendan often recalls an occasion when I had a face-to-face meeting alone with Kevin Roche, who was the Head of Light Music. The meeting turned into a massive row, and Brendan happened to be passing by in the corridor when I emerged from Kevin's office, shouting '. . . and Brendan Balfe agrees with every word I said!' before slamming the door behind me.

Arthur Murphy, a fellow broadcaster, was very often the butt of our jokes. Arthur constantly worried about his career – why he wasn't getting the good jobs, why others could take long holidays, what the world had against him generally. I told him it was because he was a Protestant and that there was a religious 'bar' in place; Brendan told him people thought he was too wealthy; and we both convinced him that Gay Byrne owned a trawler in Howth, and that he used to clean it, personally, every Saturday morning before going in to do *The Late Late Show*!

But it was John Keogh, he of Full Circle and Green Beats fame, and latterly of *The Lyrics Board*, who, in my opinion, played the best ever practical joke on radio. Liam Nolan had returned from a successful career with the BBC to present the mid-morning programme, *The Liam Nolan*

Show, on RTE radio. His style was thought by many to be overly sincere and he was very liberal with religious phrases, such as 'God bless you', during his programmes. (Mind you, I still consider Liam Nolan to be one of RTE's best ever broadcasters.) John Keogh was one of the producers on the programme. He was responsible for the second half of the programme, from twelve until a quarter to one, which was regarded as the more 'trivial' section, all the heavy stuff going into part one, between eleven and twelve. John's responsibilities were mainly musical. On this particular day, he spoke with Liam before they went on air and they decided to invite listeners to phone into the programme with their favourite joke and that they would broadcast it live.

John then told Liam a rather questionable little story about a Dublin tramp who got on a train, met a girl, offered her a bite of his sandwich, which she refused, then a smoke of his butt, which she also refused, with the ultimate tag line being 'I suppose a ride would be out of the question.' Liam, despite his image, enjoyed a smutty joke as well as anyone and thought it was hilarious.

The programme went ahead and, before twelve o'clock, Liam informed the listeners that, after the Angelus, he would be inviting listeners to phone in and go on the air 'live' with their 'favourite little joke'. He gave the telephone number and paused for the Angelus. After the Angelus, with John in the studio, Liam repeated the announcement to phone in with a favourite joke and 'who knows, we might even put you on the air'.

A few phone calls came through – knock, knock, who's there, Paddy the Irishman; harmless little things – and after a while John Keogh went missing from the control room, so there was only the technician left outside.

Another call came through and Liam said, 'And who have we here?'

'Hello, Mr Nolan,' said a deep Dublin voice that I, for one, instantly recognised as being one of the many voices of Mr Keogh. I was the continuity announcer for the morning and I promptly left the studio to go up and observe what was happening.

'Hello, Mr Nolan. This is Paddy O'Reilly from Tallaght.'

'Yes, Mr O'Reilly,' said Liam courteously. 'And have you a little joke for us?'

'Yes, Mr Nolan. I hope you enjoy this one.'

'Hopefully, too, Paddy,' said Liam.

'There was this tramp, you see, that gets on a train . . .'

Liam said, 'Eh, sorry, just a . . . Mr O'Reilly, I . . . I wonder, do I know this one?'

'You see, he sees this girl in the carriage and he says to the girl, "Would you like a bite of me sandwich?" and she says "No thanks",' continued 'Mr O'Reilly'. By this stage, Liam had gone purple with anguish. He was making cut-throat motions with his hands to indicate that he wanted this particular listener off the air, but the technician was studiously reading the racing page of the *Sun*.

'And then, Mr Nolan, d'ya know what he said? "Would you like a smoke of me butt?" "No thanks," said the girl.'

'Eh, sorry, Mr O'Reilly. I think I may know this one,' said Liam rather querulously. 'I don't know that this is entirely suitable.'

'Mr O'Reilly' carried on undeterred, however. By this time Liam was gesturing madly through the glass to try to catch the technician's, or indeed anyone's, attention, to get rid of this contributor.

'And then eventually the tramp says to the girl, "I suppose . . ." – Are you still there Mr Nolan?'

At this point Liam was sitting with his head in his hands, shaking it dolefully from side to side, knowing his career was about to go out the window for ever.

'Yes, Mr O'Reilly,' he groaned resignedly. 'Yes, Mr O'Reilly, I am.'

'"I suppose", said Mr O'Reilly again, "I suppose a *kiss* would be out of the question?"'

'Oh, very good!' said Liam, rising to his feet in acclamation. 'Very good, Mr O'Reilly! Thank you, thank you, thank you! God bless now.'

John had, of course, arranged with the technician that he would leave the studio, go into a neighbouring one, and have himself put on the air when he placed his call. It was one of the best strokes I have ever been witness to in all these years.

There were of course the usual, well-recounted, inadvertent on-air 'bloopers'. There was Una Sheehy, during the course of Hospitals Requests, coming up to the break for news at half past one, fading the record and enunciating in her best Radio Éireann voice, 'Well, patients. There, I'm afraid, we must leave Harry Belafonte with his "Hole in the Bucket".' There was John Skehan, interviewing some pop impresario about great stars he had met and discussing Sandy Shaw, the British singer who liked to perform in her bare feet, exposing as much of her long and shapely legs to the public as was decent, when John asked, quite memorably, 'Legs apart, what is she like?' Then there was myself, playing the record, 'If I Had a Hammer', for Dick Organ, a member of the Dublin Naturist Club – needless to say, this was a practical joke played upon me by a member of staff (was it that you-know-what Balfe?) Another memorable one was when Valerie McGovern, on *Morning Call*, having learned the functions of the cox in the great boat races from the sports announcer, opined to the nation how she'd love to be sitting in one of those long boats with five or six men in front of her going 'in, out'!

These, all in vaguely bad taste, were real *faux pas* that were handed on from one announcers' course to the next.

By 1968, I had become well established on radio as a member of the announcing staff. I was presenting, with some degree of popular success, the request programmes and was in demand for other types of programmes as well.

Liam Devally and Terry Wogan had effectively changed the style of presentation on Radio Éireann. Up until then, it had been formal, clipped, well enunciated and extremely reserved. Devally and Wogan introduced a far more casual, throw-away style of broadcasting, and people like myself and Brendan Balfe further developed this style. There was considerable resistance, mind you, from the many traditionalists in the organisation, and we were looked on with some disapproval for many years.

The television people offered me a pop show called *The Go-Two Show*, which I co-presented with Alma Carroll and which, I think, lasted just one season. But, in general terms, I was regarded as a 'prospect'. I stood in for Harry Thuillier once or twice on Terry Wogan's quiz programme, *Jackpot* – Harry was the announcer – and I did a few other small stand-in jobs.

One day in, I think, 1969, I was wandering through television reception when I met Kevin McDonald of the newsroom who told me that they were holding auditions for television sports announcers at that very moment and that I should try for it. I went over to where the interviews were being held and Tim O'Connor of TV sports asked me if I would be interested in going in 'straight away' and doing an off-the-cuff piece of about three minutes, into camera, on any sport I cared to choose? As it happened, the Irish rugby team had been announced that day and I had some pretty strong views on the selection, so I immediately agreed.

Within a matter of a week or so, Tim phoned me and said, 'Okay, you're on. You're starting next Sunday, on the early sports results.' Now this was pretty nerve-racking. This was cold, into-camera stuff, and I had had no experience of this type of television broadcasting. Micheál O'Hehir was the Head of Sports at the time and he called me in and told me that this was a great opportunity and that they had high hopes for me in the sports department. He wished me well and told me that he'd be watching with great interest. This was just the kind of news I *didn't* want to hear.

My father suddenly began to take an interest in my career. A sports announcer was a different thing. This had some real cachet, and, besides, he was very interested in sport in general. All of a sudden, he was asking me questions about my job.

106

Anyway, came the day and I read the sports results, very nervously I thought. But the general consensus was that, while I did appear a little nervous, I had read quite well, so within a matter of months I became a part-time member of the sports announcing staff as well as the radio announcing staff.

There were a couple of memorable incidents in my career as sports announcer. In those days, both sports and news were broadcast from the tiny Studio 3. The newsreader sat at one desk and the sportsreader sat beside him, at another desk. Charles Mitchell was the highly respected, very dignified, senior newscaster at the time and I was the less than respected junior sportsreader.

One particular evening, I came into studio and Charles informed me that it was an extremely big day for news. The then Premier of Northern Ireland, Captain Terence O'Neill, had just resigned. But Charles was equally concerned about internal matters in RTE. It seems that a new newsreader had joined and had made it very clear from the outset that he was willing to work neither at night nor at weekends. Charles was quite incensed, because these were the only times the television service broadcast. Charles was indignantly chatting away to me about this new newsreader when the signature tune for the news came on.

'Are we on the air?' I asked Charles.

'No, no, it's only a rehearsal. We're alright,' he said.

Up onto the screen came Captain Terence O'Neill, who had announced his resignation that momentous day.

'Are you sure we're not on the air?' I asked again.

'No, no, no, we're just checking the film, that's all,' and he carried on talking about the new newsreader.

Eventually, O'Neill finished, saying, '. . . and those are my reasons for resigning as Premier of Northern Ireland.'

Suddenly, the camera was on Charles, but he was sitting looking to one side, with his head in his hands, talking to me. As the camera came on to him, he said indignantly, 'Well, I think the least he could do is work the weekends.' There was a horrified moment when the entire studio realised he had been caught cold. He turned to the camera and recovered as best he could. Tom Hardiman, who was the Director General of the day, happened to be watching and immediately phoned the studio. Poor Charles was forced to make an apology about being caught unawares, as he ended the bulletin. From that day on, Charles never looked right or left or anywhere else other than into the lens of the camera, from the moment he stepped into the news studio.

Maurice O'Doherty was also a newsreader at the time and he and I had been great friends since our announcing days. At that time, the newsreader would be given the news on, say, pink paper and the sportsreader on green, to differentiate one from the other. Maurice was in the middle of reading a news bulletin when a piece of pink paper – his colour, obviously – was pushed in under the door. The floor manager picked it up, folded it, rushed it over to me and indicated that I should pass it urgently to Maurice.

This I did, as Maurice intoned in his highly distinctive voice, 'Today the Vietcong crossed the demilitarised zone. Oh, excuse me one moment,' he added, reaching for the piece of paper. 'I've just been handed a newsflash.'

He read from the paper, 'In table tennis today, Trinity beat UCD by 5 matches to 4.'

There was a shocked silence and then the rest of us in the studio collapsed in silent but hysterical laughter. Maurice, however, had to complete the bulletin, which he did – manfully. However, he had his revenge. When I went on air to read the sports results, Maurice climbed under my desk and proceeded to take off my shoes and socks. Those were heady days, I can tell you!

It was around this time that Denis Meehan died from cancer. Denis had been in and out of hospital and we all thought he was in remission, but the disease finally won out. It was a very sad time for many of us. We had the deepest affection for Denis and, certainly in my case, he was instrumental in setting me on my way. He was gregarious, compassionate and, all-in-all, a delightful man. Also he had a very creative and pragmatic view of broadcasting. He could see the trends, he was keen to bring in broadcasters of the style of Wogan, Andy O'Mahony, myself, Brendan Balfe and so on – people who had a spark of personality and didn't conform to the heretofore accepted standard of Radio Éireann announcers.

When Denis died, his wife Sylvia was left with five children to bring up. But Sylvia was a fighter. She became one of the foremost members of the Women's Movement and, in fact, eventually became the leading woman trade unionist in Ireland. She is a cool, determined, highly intellectual woman, and she had a really good relationship with her husband.

Denis Meehan was the first man in my life to have a profound beneficial influence upon me. The second was about to make his appearance.

Tom McGrath was at that time 'the man'. He had come back from Canada, where he had worked in television 'from the ground up', as he used to say. He was headhunted for the opening of RTE television and had quickly established himself as the strongest personality in the station. He created *The Late Late Show*, *The Life of O'Reilly* and *Jackpot*. He produced and directed the first live TV drama, *Flight into Danger*, he took charge of all drama and light entertainment programmes and, all-in-all, he was the single greatest influence on television broadcasting for all of the sixties and much of the seventies.

Tom was a forceful, burly, strong-minded, often contrary, stubborn and very humorous man, who created as many enemies for himself as he did friends. He was legendary in the business for his single-mindedness and abrasiveness; his 'nobody stops the show but me' rang out through the talk-back system before every programme he directed. He allowed nobody – floor manager, lighting director, sound technician – to stop a show once the red light went on. His priority was always the performer and the effect of the performance on the audience.

Tom was one of only two producer/directors I have worked with (the other being John McColgan) who had the ability to 'watch' television while making it. Tom used his own mother as his touchstone, an old-fashioned precept it seems now, but at that time it made a lot of sense. As he was 'watching' television he could put himself into the place of his mother, who he believed was a good common denominator for the Irish viewer, and he would determine there and then whether it was good television or whether it was pretentious. There were many who saw Tom's view of TV as simplistic, but Tom never compromised his views and he certainly did create some of the more memorable moments in Irish broadcasting.

In 1970, Dana won the Eurovision Song Contest for Ireland and, as a result, the following year we were to stage the Eurovision Song Contest in the Gaiety Theatre in Dublin. Early in 1971, I received a phone call from a member of Tom's staff inviting me to call into the Francis Xavier Hall, or SFX as it is now known, where Tom was rehearsing the orchestra. I was taken aback by the request. I knew Tom by reputation – a pretty fearsome reputation – and I had bumped into him once or twice at record receptions, but I didn't think he would remember me.

I went along at the appointed time and sat at the back of the auditorium, while Tom was at the front working with Noel Kelehan, I think it was, on arrangements for the orchestra. After a while, he turned and sauntered back down the hall towards me. Tom was over six feet tall, heavy-set, always smoked a pipe, wore glasses and walked in a slow, deliberate manner, with a hint of a swagger. He sat down on the arm of the chair on the other side of the aisle and took his pipe from his mouth.

'Howya, head? I've seen you a coupla times on the sports programmes and I've heard a few of your request programmes, and I'd like to ask you to present this year's National Song Contest on TV.'

I left the hall, walked out into the street and, about two hundred yards down the road, leapt into the air with joy. This was the big one and I knew it. This was make or break time for me, and I was confident that I would be able to handle it well. A year or two afterwards, Tom told me how surprised he was at the coolness of my reaction. He said that my expression never changed, that I simply thanked him, shook hands with him, and left. He didn't even know whether I was pleased or not!

On the big night of the National Song Contest, I was extremely nervous. Eileen was in the audience, enjoying this, her first big night in terms of my career. Our three girls, Elaine, Carol and our latest, Deirdre, were watching at home with Gran. I got through the show quite well and there was a favourable reaction afterwards. Let me not minimise the pressure that was involved, though. I was sick with nerves. At this time, the National Song Contest and *The Late Late Show* were the big programmes, the National Song Contest always capturing one of the biggest audiences of the year. And, naturally, Tom and RTE had capitalised, in terms of publicity, on the choice of the new young compère, so I was literally under a microscope. But, when it was over, I knew that it had gone well.

For some months afterwards I continued to read the sports results, on a part-time basis, along with my other part-time colleague, Paddy O'Neill, who was also famous, under the name Paddy O'Brien, as Ireland's leading greyhound commentator. Paddy, who unfortunately has since died, was a Corkman with a puckish sense of humour and was, as he would have said himself, 'doing very nicely' at the time. He was employed on the production staff of RTE radio, was reading sports results on television and, as I mentioned, he also had his greyhound commentaries. I said to him that we ought to ask Micheál O'Hehir for an increase in our pay for the sports results. He was adamantly opposed to my suggestion.

'No, don't rock the boat. The secret is not to let them know you're still here. If they think you're going to create a fuss, they'll just get rid of you.'

I told Paddy that I didn't agree and that I was going to see Micheál about it in any case.

'Well, you're not to associate me with your request for more money. Leave me as I am. I'm fine,' said Paddy.

So I went in to see Micheál, who, as usual, was gracious and welcoming. He sat me down and asked me what my problem was. I told him I had no problem, but that I could do with extra money, as five guineas a night – for a Sunday, first of all, and for both early and late sports results – seemed to me a bit low.

'Oh, you really think so, do you?' he said.

'Well, I do, actually.'

'And are you speaking on behalf of Paddy and yourself?' he asked.

'No,' I said. 'Paddy specifically asked me *not* to associate him with my request.'

'How much do you think you should be getting?'

'I think it should be doubled,' I said.

'You want ten guineas?'

'Well, I think it should be pounds as well. I think you should round it off to eleven pounds.'

'Do you?' he said.

'I do.'

'Very well then. I think you're right. I think you're underpaid, so I will increase it and let's agree on eleven pounds,' and we shook hands on it.

When I emerged from the office, Paddy happened to be waiting nearby. He asked me how it had gone, so I told him, but I also said that I had been very careful to dissociate him from any request for extra money and so he would remain on his current rate. Paddy was extremely disconcerted, and it took him, according to Mick O'Hehir, a month to pluck up the courage to ask for the same rate as I was getting.

Elaine and Carol as adorable little girls — they still are!

By the time Eileen and I visited Washington in 1975, Declan was well established there and even had his own car parking space on Capitol Hill!

My first professional acting role with Colette Dunne — and the first occasion I was known as 'Mike'. That's Kevin Redmond who, as Julius Caesar, got stabbed for real by me in our days in the Dublin Shakespeare Society.

Cool, calm and tone deaf —
immortalised on vinyl.
Release Records were lucky
enough to have one or two
copies of the L.P. left over
after the initial rush!

There was a technician in Radio Eireann many years ago who, when sent to record Mass in country churches for radio, would enter the building, clap his hands, wait for the reverberation and mutter, 'My problem is I'm a perfectionist — I'm cursed with perfect pitch'. My own sentiments exactly as I laid down the tracks for my L.P.!

1969. Brendan Balfe and myself trying a sip of neat honey on one of our legendary 'Hotel Crawls'.

The Dublin Festival Company on its way to take Paris by ..... breeze.
Samuel Beckett couldn't find enough negatives to heap on this gallant troupe.

Left to right: (Front row) Maureen Hurley, Jackie MacGowran, Brendan Smith,
Ronnie Masterson, Ray MacAnally, Eamonn Morrisey; (Back row) D. Hill,
May Cluskey, May MacFaul, Dermot Tuohy; (On airplane steps) Michael
Campion, Beryl Fagan, Eithne Lydon, Fred Johnson, myself, David Kelly,
Marie Murphy, Anne Brogan, Derek Young, Kay Johnson, Brid Ni Loinnsigh.

In the late '70s Actors Equity went on strike. On duty that day were (*left to right*): newsreader Cyril Smyth, actress Colette Proctor, myself and actor Peadar Lamb.

'Live' radio in Cork with that fine figure of Leeside masculinity, Danny La Rue.

Among some special people on Benedict Kiely's birthday. *Left to right :* Ciarán Mac Mathúna, Sean J White, Peter Brown, myself, Benedict, John Ryan and Frank Murphy, our colourful researcher.

My old and much valued pal, Geno — Gene Martin.

Tom McGrath.

Nashville. Tammy Wynette gets the RTE 'Sound Man' treatment from Brian Lynch. I could have stuck the microphone in my left ear for all he cared.

Nero looking a little nervous while the lion-tamer appears masterful and not to be trifled with.

Likes of Mike — sky-divin',
shootin', swimmin'.

Father Trendy — sorry, Ted, sorry,
Dermot — at my 40th birthday.

Critic Fodder

I had by now decided it was time to try my luck in the freelance world. We had moved house from our small first home in Ballinteer to Kerrymount Rise in Foxrock. To my mother and father, this was an act of sheer madness. The house was £8,150, a small fortune then, and I wasn't in that kind of wage bracket. However, I went ahead.

We had been concerned about Eileen's mother living on her own in her home in Orwell Gardens in Rathgar, so I suggested she should move in with us. She was almost seventy years old and was beginning to feel her age. So she joined us in 1969 and remained with us for the following sixteen years, until her death in 1985. She and I got on extremely well and she often used to boast about the fact that, in all the years we lived together, she and I never had a single row.

I grew to love Gran and she did her very best to allow us our privacy in the home. But, at this remove, were I to be asked if it is a good idea for an elderly parent to move in with a young family, I think I would have to say 'no'. It meant that, for all those years, the home was run by two competent women, so the children were expected to do little or nothing for themselves in the house. Gran was also old-fashioned in that, when I came home, it was a case of the 'man of the house' arriving; his dinner should be ready, the kids should be out of the way and he should be able to relax after a hard day's work. So a certain distance was created between myself and the family during those years.

I had been, however, somewhat trepidatious about marriage and family, after my own experiences at home, and I was utterly determined that my children would never suffer the kind of grey, dismal, destructive atmosphere to which I had been subjected. So I did my best to create a jovial and cheerful family home. In retrospect, I think that this may not always have been the right way to handle things. My workload was extremely heavy. I was playing charity football with the Jimmy McGee All-Stars, I attended functions, I worked unearthly hours – early mornings and late nights – but when I was at home, I tried to create as light-hearted an atmosphere as possible. So, my children never saw me depressed, never were aware of the problems I was encountering in my work, never saw me as anything but cheerful, competent and in control. Eileen was a good and totally dedicated mother, and she, too, tried to insulate the children from any discomfort.

After a few years, I bought a lovely little stone house in Glenmalure, County Wicklow. Eamon Morrissey and myself had always promised ourselves that some day we would live in County Wicklow. Eamon had bought an old ruin in Aghavannagh and I, among others, had helped him to rebuild it into a very pleasant weekend home. Glenmalure was in the next valley and so, when I saw the ad in the *Irish Times*, I rushed down to the estate agent and immediately put in a bid of £6,500 for it.

We spent the next year doing up the cottage and for many years after we wended our way down to Glenmalure for the weekend. It was a beautiful place to visit, the scenery was wonderful, the neighbours were delightful and we grew to love the lifestyle there. However, as the years passed, the children became less and less enthusiastic about travelling down every weekend and I eventually sold the house.

We were becoming quite the 'glamorous couple' by now, very much in demand socially, with all the outward appearances of happiness and success. But I am inclined to feel now that we made it all seem too easy to our children. If children don't see the effort that their parents have to make, it is easy for them to perceive success and happiness as theirs by right. We didn't address the serious questions sufficiently, in their lives or ours. We tried to make it appear that the sun shone all day and every day. It seems ironic that parents, in trying to do the right thing by their children, sheltering them from hurt and disappointment, can in fact build for them a false premise on which to construct their lives.

It seems to me that the dice are loaded against good parenting. The way our lives are structured in this society can cheat us of the opportunity to get it right. The years between twenty-five and thirty-five, when one is building a career, coincide precisely with the years in which one is most needed by partner and children. This, I believe, is why many men, in particular, reach their late forties and enjoy being around young children and why they dote on their grandchildren, often to the surprise and possible resentment of their own family.

Around this time, RTE decided that some of their radio presenters needed to brush up their Irish in a very serious way, so they inaugurated Irish classes for us. For most of the announcing staff this was a breeze, as most of them had a good smattering of Irish, but for me there was considerable trauma involved.

Anyway, I went along to the classes and found myself paired with veteran broadcaster Joe Linnane, who, like me, was 'linguistically deprived'. Joe, in fact, was even worse than I was, but he managed to latch on to the Irish word for an ashtray, which was *luaithreadán*, and one or two other little phrases as well.

When RTE in their wisdom decided to send some of us to the Gaeltacht to study the language at first hand, Joe and I were dispatched to Ballyferriter in County Kerry. We packed our golf clubs, in case we needed to play golf in Irish as well, and off we headed.

When we arrived in Ballyferriter, we pulled up at the first *teach tábhairne* we encountered, which turned out to be Donal Ó Catháin's place. It was a fairly dull day and Joe, being the more masterful – brash, some might say – entered the pub first. A number of locals were sitting in relative silence at the counter as we entered.

'*Dia dhíbh a dhaoine uaisle,*' announced Joe, lavishly.

'*Ar Dia bhúr mbeatha*', replied Donal Ó Catháin and followed that up with a *ceist*, or question. This totally flummoxed Joe. He ignored the *ceist*, looked up and down the counter, and then addressed an elderly gentleman in a grey cap at the far end of the bar.

'*A dhuine uasal,*' he said, confidently, '*Tabhair dom an luaithreadán, le do thoil.*' The man, who seemed a little startled at being addressed in the first place, looked around and murmured, '*Cad é?*'

'*An luaithreadán,*' said Joe, in his best broadcasting voice. '*An luaithreadán, le do thoil.*'

'*Níl fhios agam cad é sin,*' said the man, plainly embarrassed.

'*An luaithreadán,*' insisted Joe, miming taking a cigarette from his mouth and stubbing it out on the counter. '*An luaithreadán. Ansan.*'

'Ohhh,' said the man, the light dawning, '*An t-ashtray,*' and passed the ashtray up to Joe. Joe was dumbfounded.

'Did you hear what he just said?' he said to me. '*An t-ashtray.*' He was shattered. 'I could have told him that meself.'

That was the end of the Irish course for Joe. The next day we headed off for County Clare, where we played a few rounds of golf at Lahinch and then made our disconsolate way back to Dublin.

A few months after the National Song Contest, Tom McGrath contacted me and asked me to meet him for a drink. He asked me if I had thought about presenting my own television series. I said no, I certainly had not.

'Well, I have an idea for a series that I think will interest you,' he said.

'It will involve games, some singing and some dancing.'

I looked askance. Of course, I had already recorded the LP with Wogan's imprimatur (if you could call it that) on the sleeve, but the record had disappeared without trace. However, whether I liked it or not, it was still on my c.v. and Tom knew it. As regards dancing, I had for a few weeks, when I was in the Brendan Smith Academy, attended Spanish dancing classes run by a Mr Desmond Domican who ran a studio in Parnell Square. Mr Domican, a single man who lived with his mother, thought that some of my fellow thespians were a lot more talented than me at the terpsichorean arts and, on two Sundays in a row, prevailed upon me to walk his three white poodles around Parnell Square while the others learned how to dance with castanets. So my dancing career wasn't that promising. But Tom was insistent.

'I can show you how to get away with it,' he said, 'and I think you have the talent to carry your own show. So let me do the worrying about that.' I had more than a few niggling doubts, but I decided to trust Tom's instincts, and so we set to work.

Tom made great demands on my time.

'If you're not prepared to dedicate all your time and energy to this project, then tell me now and we'll forget the whole thing. I want your total commitment.'

I told him he could have it. My total commitment that is. To Tom, 'total commitment' meant every spare moment. When we were not actually working, we were discussing and agonising over the project. Usually in a pub. Tom was drinking very heavily and I began drinking to keep him company. We met with various people, including Cecil Sheridan and Danny Cummins, in order to devise games; we auditioned dancers; we listened to singers male and female; we went to comedy shows, cabarets and concerts together. It was, as he had said, 'total commitment'.

Within a few months, we had put the package together, had decided to call the programme *The Likes of Mike* and had selected the cast. There was the young comedian and impressionist, David Beggs, who was to

125

have topical scripts written for him by Donal Foley, the author of the satirical column, 'Man Bites Dog', in the *Irish Times*. There was Brian Hoey, a tenor, making his début as (and Tom came up with these pretty cringe-making captions) 'Mike's buddy'. And there was Alma Carroll, the singer I had known for many years and with whom I had co-presented *The Go-Two Show*, who was billed (quite unthinkable nowadays) as 'Mike's girlfriend'. How I agreed to these captions, I'll never know! Here was I, a happily married father of three, making my television début with an attractive girl singer dubbed 'Mike's girlfriend'. God, the goosepimples!

The Likes of Mike was billed – along with Dana's new show – as the highlight of RTE's new autumn schedule. Tom and I were in Castlebar, where he was directing and I was presenting the Castlebar Song Contest, when the first show was transmitted. It was a Friday night and local reaction was mixed. Some people were very complimentary to me and others were simply polite, while one or two were pretty forthright in voicing their criticism.

Driving back to Dublin on the Sunday morning, we bought the Sunday newspapers to check the reviews. They were, quite simply, awful. At that time, newspaper coverage of television programmes was quite disproportionate to their importance. Large headlines like 'Murphy's TV Show a Disaster' and 'Give it up Mike' were followed by long negative reviews by the critics. I was sick with dismay and disappointment – and also fear. How would I face people? How would I walk into RTE the next day? How would I continue with the rest of the series? How would I face the people we had engaged and who were contracted to complete the series? I just wanted to get home, crawl into bed and disappear from the face of the earth.

Tom, however, took control. He told me that every person who ever achieved any form of public prominence would, at some stage in their career, undergo such a barrage of criticism. He said that, in many ways, I was lucky that it had happened so early in my professional life, because I would be able to derive strength from coping with it and it would help me with similar situations in the future. He told me that, for the sake of all the other people involved, I had to put on a brave face.

'Remember this,' he said. 'You have access to the most powerful medium in the country. There are more people watching you on television at any one time than there are reading any of those newspaper columns.'

He advised me not to react in a hostile way to my critics.

'Don't even acknowledge their presence. Never let them see that you're hurt. Rise above the whole thing.'

He told me that I must never allow a newspaper columnist, a critic, or anyone to deter me from doing what I believed was right for me.

By the time we reached Dublin, Tom had managed to put some semblance of steel back into my spine. Eileen also did her best to cheer me up and, the next day, I squared my shoulders, held my head high and went into RTE for rehearsal. I have never, that day or since, showed any reaction to criticism, favourable or otherwise.

Kevin Marron – the late and much lamented Kevin Marron – who died tragically some years later in an air accident, was the clever and irreverent TV critic of the new *Sunday World* newspaper, and he was the most savage of all in terms of *The Likes of Mike*. But his saving grace was that he was extremely funny about it, and although I smarted and cringed at the comments Kevin made about me Sunday after Sunday, I couldn't help but allow myself to smile at his invention and clever turn of phrase.

One week, however, after Kevin had been particularly scathing about me, I received a phone call from him later in the week. He told me that he had received a note from my daughter, Elaine, in which she had referred to him as a 'bitch'. Elaine was then no more than six or seven years of age and she had taken it upon herself, after reading Kevin's column, to write to him, get a stamp and post the letter. She didn't know what a 'bitch' was, she just knew it was a bad word and so chose to use it. Kevin was very upset about the letter and, in fact, so was I. He told me that he would drop a line to Elaine and he asked me to try to explain to her that much of what he wrote was done in jest, and even with some affection.

Over the years, in spite our professional differences, Kevin and I became very close friends and he subsequently presented me with a birthday present of a framed caricature of me from the *Sunday World*, with one of his smart-ass captions underneath. But he inscribed it with 'To Mike, with deep affection, Kevin'. Some years later, he and I were to write a joint column for the *Sunday World* about my first trip to the United States.

I was, however, greatly amused by an incident in Madigan's pub during that first run of *The Likes of Mike*. I was with some friends and family, sitting with my back to the room, when I sensed rather than saw a gent, who was somewhat under the weather, weaving his way towards me. The conversation stopped as he stood beside me and tapped me on the shoulder.

'Hey,' he said. 'Do you be on the telly, do ya?'

'I do, that's right,' I said, turning round. He tapped me again on the shoulder.

'Well, I wanna tell ya,' he said truculently, 'I think you're fuckin' brutal.'

I was taken aback, but managed to say, 'Oh, well, there you are, you can't please all of the people . . .' or some such inane comment. He surveyed the rest of the company for a moment, then turned his attention back to me, tapping me once again on the shoulder.

'Hey.'

'Yes,' I said, cringing.

'You think I'm fuckin' jokin', don't ya? Well, I'm not.'

I told him I knew by the way he had walked over that he was a very sincere person and I was aware that there wasn't a humorous bone in his body. He turned as if to go. No such luck! He had remembered something else. Once again, he tapped me on the shoulder.

'Hey,' he said, 'An' another thing . . .'

'What?' I mumbled.

'The wife fuckin' hates ya, too.' A pause. 'An' she knows fuck all.' There was no possible recovery from that. I was left for dead.

There were other critics less talented and more vicious than Kevin Marron to whom I didn't take at all. I probably choose not to remember some of the more vicious things said or written about me, but I do recall being deeply offended by Tom O'Dea, in the *Irish Press*, when he referred to me as a 'mere marshmallow'. That hurt, and I disliked O'Dea for being so downright insulting to somebody he had never even met.

Television and radio criticism at that time was often low on the list of priorities of a newspaper editor. That the 'alternative' media needed to be catered for somewhere in print was accepted, but the quality of the criticism was often questionable. In fact, this practice hasn't totally died out – there are still some pretty awful TV and radio columns around. One in particular, in a current Sunday newspaper, springs to mind, which, when it isn't 'postponed until next week due to lack of space', is often a rehash of quotes from *The Gerry Ryan Show*, or a sycophantic doff in the general direction of Marian Finucane, or an attempt to imitate Joe Duffy's accent in print. It shows no originality whatsoever and is utterly devoid of wit. I don't mean to offend Tom Widger, but, as I recall, he wouldn't be too sensitive about criticising others in print.

However, if I were to avail myself of this opportunity to air a view or two about critics, I would have to reserve ninety per cent of my scorn and spleen for Colm Tóibín, who has since become a fairly successful novelist. In the 1980s, a column appeared in *Magill* magazine, written by a name I didn't recognise, which dealt viciously, savagely and insultingly with my professional life and personality. It was devastatingly cruel and deeply wounding. A lot of people were, like myself, astounded by the savagery of the attack. Eamon Dunphy's more recent attack on Pat Kenny was pretty tame by comparison.

At that time I was presenting a daytime radio programme, and one of my regular contributors was Colm Tóibín, who would come in to talk about books. For some weeks after the article in question had appeared, Tóibín continued to come into the studio and do his piece, we would have some desultory conversation and he would go. Eventually, Colin Morrison, who was producer at the time, spoke to me.

'How can you be so pleasant to that man after what he has done to you?'

I asked him what he meant and he told me that Tóibín had been the author of that piece in *Magill*. A few nights later, I was at the Gaiety Theatre with Eileen and I spotted Tóibín sitting with Fintan O'Toole of the *Irish Times* a few rows below me. In the interval, I beckoned him across. I then proceeded to tell him what I thought of him: that he was a craven hypocrite, that he had deeply insulted both myself and my family, that I equated him with the archetypal school sneak, and that I considered him to be a worthless individual of no principle. I told him that I wouldn't have been so outraged had he written the column under his own name, but to write it under an assumed name was an act of cowardice. That was the only time I ever responded to anything that had been written about me. In terms of Tóibín's future, one thing is certain. He will not appear with me in any studio over which I have control.

I currently enjoy A A Gill's TV column in the *Sunday Times*. Sometimes he is biting, often savage, but never less than entertaining. I'm thankful that I am not one of his targets, but, even if I was, I couldn't help but admire the style with which he applies the dagger.

In my opinion, Eddie Holt, who is currently writing for the *Irish Times*, is also developing into a very good, astute and entertaining critic. But I can hardly suppress a grin as I imagine the reactions of the various self-important TV and radio critics, who would feel diminished and very offended were I, or someone like me, to review their work as they review mine. Methinks many of them would prove to be very delicate flowers indeed!

Death of a Matriarch

Tom was right. *The Likes of Mike* survived on air for the next few years, despite the Controller of Programmes, Michael Garvey, taking Tom to one side one day and saying to him, in all seriousness, 'Would it not be a good idea if Mike took some dancing lessons?'

'But Michael,' said Tom, 'Don't you understand? That's the joke — that Mike *can't dance*.'

Michael was, understandably, a little bemused. But people got used to the series and it did incredibly well in the ratings, vying each week with *The Late Late Show* for the number one spot.

The toll on my family life was, however, quite significant. Tom demanded most of my time and I went along with him, which meant that there were many late nights in pubs. I would meet Tom for a pint every Saturday evening and Sunday morning. This was the pattern of our lives.

After a third year of the series, Tom said to me, 'Okay, head, it's time you went your own way and I went mine.' So, our intense working and personal relationship ceased. We did work together again on another series some years later, and Tom remained, until his death, one of my best friends.

Tom is remembered by many for his idiosyncrasies. We, the cast, the band and the technical staff, would have adjourned to Madigan's in Donnybrook for our tea break, and Tom would tell us that the dress rehearsal would begin 'at seven-thirty sharp'. We would all sit together, laughing, joking, slagging and generally having a good time – Tom, Earl Gill, John Curran, Desi Reynolds, Annie Bushnell, Des Moore, John Drummond, Pat Reilly, Alma Carroll, David Beggs, Jerry Hughes, Brian Hoey, and so on. (Earl was the leader of the band at the time.) At twenty-five past seven, Tom would throw back the remains of his drink, stand up and, without a word, would walk out the door.

He would drive straight back to RTE, walk up to the control room, sit down in the director's chair and, at seven-thirty precisely, would instruct the floor manager to cue the band. The floor manager, bemused, would say, 'But Tom, they're not here yet.'

'I don't care,' Tom would say. 'Cue the band.'

'Tom, there's no band here.'

'Cue the band,' Tom would insist. 'They're supposed to be here at half past seven.'

By now the band would have begun to straggle into the studio. Tom would come out to the gantry, look down and say, 'Where were you?'

'We were with you, Tom.'

'Yeah, but why weren't you here on time?'

'But Tom, you left early.'

'That's your problem. It's your job to be here at seven-thirty on the dot and I don't care how you get here, as long you do.'

It was stories like this that created the legend around Tom.

On another occasion, Tom and myself and a crew had been dispatched to Tralee during the Rose of Tralee festival to make a documentary about the festival itself. Brian MacLochlann had made a documentary that showed a very uncomplimentary view of life in Tralee and its environs, so we were sent down to redress the balance and make a nice gentle documentary that would reflect all that was good, sincere and decent about Tralee and the festival.

Tom decided that we would film these beautiful young girls from all over the world, the Roses, while they were at prayer. So he told the crew, including me, 'I want to see you all at mass tomorrow at half past nine. That's when the Roses will be there.'

So we all duly turned up at nine-thirty. I knelt about a third of the way down the church, while Tom, who had by now taken to wearing a red anorak, open-toed sandals and pink sunglasses, beckoned to the crew to follow him to the altar. The priest knew nothing of our arrival and was somewhat bemused by the strange assortment of people standing at the altar to his right. The cameraman, Godfrey Graham, was mortified. He kept his eyes lowered and a gentle blush suffused his features. I looked on with morbid fascination while Tom directed the lighting man to go hunting around the altar for an electric socket into which he could plug the lights. The priest was well into the mass at this stage, the Roses were in the first two pews of the church and Tom was completely unselfconscious, standing casually throughout most of the ceremony. However, when the moment came for the priest to distribute Holy Communion, Tom sauntered across, stopped him in mid-step as he made his way down to the altar rails and said, 'Excuse me, Father. Could you hold it just there for a moment, please?'

The priest froze. As is usual in Catholic churches, every little old lady in the community had rushed forward to be first to receive Communion, and the altar rails were thronged. Tom, leaving the priest suspended, walked down and said to the little old ladies, 'Excuse me, would you all mind stepping back and letting the Roses come forward?'

The denizens of Tralee dutifully stepped back, while the Roses were welcomed to the altar rails by this strange figure in pink sunglasses. When the Roses were comfortably installed, Tom took the priest by the elbow, indicated to Godfrey to stand at the priest's other side and then guided the priest to the far end of the rails. He instructed Godfrey to crouch down and edge backwards as the priest moved along the line, so that the girls could be seen by their various families in the act of receiving the sacrament. Godfrey was bright purple at this stage.

'I don't think so, Tom,' he mumbled, 'I really don't think so.'

Tom overruled him with a forceful 'Godfrey, just do it!' Then he turned to the priest and said, 'Okay, Father, take it from here and go right along the line, slowly. Thank you very much.'

And thus were all thirty-two Roses that year commemorated on film as being in a state of grace! As I crouched down in the body of the church (hoping that no one would recognise me, or at least if they did would think I was working on a different programme). I couldn't help but notice that all thirty-two of them had felt sufficiently intimidated to receive Holy Communion. It struck me that probably not all of them were Catholics, and that it was even less likely that all of them were in a state of grace at the time. But the wishes of the Great Controller (Tom) had prevailed.

For many people, the story that epitomised the nature of Tom's personality was the famous night of the first Eurovision Song Contest to be staged in Dublin – in 1970 at the Gaiety Theatre, as I have mentioned before. The dress rehearsal over, Tom had gone across the road for a drink and returned to the theatre ten minutes before transmission. That was his style. He never got flustered, never got excited, never overreacted; he was unbelievably cool, even at such an important event. At the theatre door, the security man refused him entry because he was not wearing any accreditation.

'I never wear those things,' said Tom, 'I'm the director of the show.'

'I'm sorry,' said the security man, 'You're not gaining admittance. You don't have the correct accreditation.'

'Fine,' said Tom. 'If anybody's looking for Tom McGrath, tell them he'll be across in Rice's pub,' and he promptly walked off and returned to the pub.

Inside the Gaiety, there was consternation. Where was Tom? Where was the director? Somebody said they had seen him in the pub a few minutes earlier and somebody else was dispatched to get him. Tom was sitting calmly reading the *Evening Herald* and smoking his pipe when he was found.

'Tom! There's only six minutes to go!' the emissary said.

'Well, I'm afraid I won't be with you. I don't have the necessary accreditation.'

The emissary rushed out, the head of security was dragged back to the pub and, three minutes (and no more) from air time, the director calmly sat in his chair to broadcast one of the best ever Eurovisions around the world.

I have mentioned the Rose of Tralee festival. Last year, when Gay Byrne was taken ill, the Director of Television, Liam Miller, contacted me and asked if I would stand in for Gay. I told him that I had no time for the Rose of Tralee concept and that it would be an act of hypocrisy on my part to present the show. Liam, however, said he would deem it a personal favour if I would overcome my reservations and do the show. I very reluctantly agreed, put the phone down, remembered something and called him back.

'Liam,' I said, 'I'm terribly sorry, but I'm not going to be able to do the show, because I'll be recording the entire series of *Up and Running* on the days I would be required in Tralee.'

Miller, who happens to be one of the most talented and well-rounded executives that RTE has been fortunate enough to have, thanked me for agreeing despite my reservations and contacted Derek Davis, who was pleased to take over and who did a superb job – much better than I would have done.

I really don't like the Rose of Tralee contest. It represents to me everything that is hypocritical and smug about this country. It is the glossy clingfilm that enfolds the last vestiges of de Valera's Ireland. The young women are stereotypical and the organisers are careful to keep them within very narrow parameters. Maidenly, sweet, contented with life, with love, with their jobs, living blissful family lives with loving parents and adoring siblings, wishing always to return to their roots in Ireland, and particularly to be part of the hospitality and spirit of the

Rose of Tralee festival. I yearn for one of these young women to say that she is a lesbian, that she is long-term unemployed, that she approves of divorce, that she has been involved in an unhappy affair with a married man, that her family have had problems with alcohol; that real life, as most of us know it, could penetrate into this hollow Shangri La. I don't mean that people should expose their innermost secrets, I just mean that I am ill at ease with the cosy smugness of this annual, semi-religious bash. Let someone come out and admit that it is a purely commercial exercise and I will applaud, but purveying this particular Irish feminine ideal is a line that I, for one, don't buy.

Even as recently as last April, the Rose of Tralee committee announced that single mothers categorically will not be, nor ever were, acceptable contestants in their competition. Need I say more?

On a Friday in 1975, I was rehearsing *The Likes of Mike* for live transmission that night, when I received a phone call to the studio. It was my sister Pat, who informed me that my mother had been involved in a slight accident, but not to worry, she was going to be fine. I went straight upstairs to the control room and told Tom the message exactly as I had received.

'Go this minute to your mother. I'll handle everything here,' he said.

I got into the car and drove home to Vernon Grove, where my father, Pat and John were seated around the kitchen. My mother had been crossing the road to go to ten o'clock mass in Rathgar Church, as she did every morning, when a young man on a motorcycle had, seemingly, lost control of his bike and crashed into her, throwing her a good distance in the air and onto the footpath. She had head injuries and was unconscious when the ambulance arrived and took her to the Meath Hospital.

The family was now waiting for news of the emergency operation she was undergoing, and had been told to remain at home. We all sat around stunned, trying to offer each other solace and encouragement.

Finally, we could stand it no longer and, leaving Da, who didn't want to come, in Pat's company, John and I went down to the hospital.

We waited for some time before my mother was wheeled out of the operating theatre. She was heavily bandaged and unconscious. John took her hand and murmured something to her and she was wheeled on past us. John said afterwards that she distinctly squeezed his hand when she heard his voice. The surgeon told us that she was very seriously injured, that she had some brain damage and that it was pointless for us to wait at the hospital. He said that he would be with her all the time and he would prefer she had no visitors.

So we went home and sat around again, fearing the worst. Within a couple of hours, the phone call came. She had died without regaining consciousness. My father put his head in his hands and sobbed. We did our best to comfort one other. We tried to remain active. At difficult times like that, you want to feel that you can do something that will make things better, as distinct from simply acknowledging that someone you care about is gone.

I phoned Catherine in Spain and Declan in the United States to give them the bad news and then we went through all the usual formalities. It was a huge funeral, and Declan came over to say the mass. He, like the rest of us, was distraught, and I recall the poor fellow breaking down as he said mass. The church was thronged. The TV show had been cancelled and there was attendant publicity, and I can recall my own surprise when I emerged from the church behind my mother's coffin to see the Taoiseach of the day, Jack Lynch, standing in the crowd. The father of the young man who had killed her was standing to one side and, when he caught my eye, he rushed over, put his arms round my neck and sobbed on my shoulder.

She had been a remarkably strong-willed, indefatigable woman of her time. She knew what she wanted and was determined to get her way. As with all true individuals, there was the good and the bad, the admirable and the difficult about her – and my mother certainly was a highly individualistic woman. I owe her a great deal, as do my brothers and sisters. On the negative side, she was manipulative, attention-seeking and often quite ruthless and divisive when it suited her. On the positive side, she taught us to be constructive and optimistic, to open our eyes to possibility and to the wonders of the world, and to face difficulties with courage and determination.

A coroner's inquest was held. I attended with my father and Pat. The lawyers, coroner and other chief protagonists were muttering to each other at the head of the courtroom and we could not properly hear what they were saying, although I did catch them referring to my mother as 'the old lady'. She was only 62, for God's sake! I became irritated. I stood up in the court and asked them all to 'kindly stop mumbling to themselves' and to 'speak up, as there were no more interested parties in the room than ourselves and we couldn't hear what was being said'. It worked! Suddenly they were all orators.

My father remained at Vernon Grove for a number of years afterwards. John was still at home, after enjoying a hugely pleasurable six months in Spain, and had gone into the motor business with my father. Da didn't really appreciate John, and he made a lot of demands on him that John quietly acceded to. John functioned as his driver and his messenger, but, although my brother was bright and efficient, Da generally seemed to have little respect for him.

It was a curious trait of my father's, all through the years, that he would more or less 'adopt' young men of our age who worked for him, probably because he himself had been deprived of a relationship with his own sons. I recall being extremely jealous of a young mechanic named Frankie who travelled everywhere with my father and about whom my father, when he was in good form, would rave. Later, there was another young man, named John McInerney, who became the focus of my father's attentions and, again, he was all the things that his own sons should have been.

This pattern continued when my brother John was working with Da. John became quite disillusioned and decided to go into the clothing business on his own. This almost led to bankruptcy, however, and so he began selling insurance. He used to get the bus across to Donaghmede and walk from house to house all day long, trying to sell from door to door. I was full of admiration for John who, having failed a couple of times, was now, in his early to mid-twenties, literally pounding the pavements, trying to make a few bob. Within a few years, his diligence and intelligence paid off and he rose through the ranks of corporate insurance in this city and is now General Manager at Friends' Provident with a wonderful job, a lovely wife, Lisanne, and three beautiful daughters – Kim, who is my goddaughter, Sara and Samantha.

Auntie May, loyal, lovable Auntie May, had by now moved into 'digs' in Rathgar, and it was she who came in on a regular basis to cook and wash for my father. She did it cheerfully and I believe she was genuinely very fond of him and he of her.

My Kingdom for a Horse,
or a Lion, or a Coffin

Although Tom McGrath and I had parted company professionally (and temporarily as it turned out) RTE wanted me to do another series of *The Likes of Mike*. So I began to think about producers. I have always worked on the basis that I work best myself if in tandem with a producer whose work I admire and whose company I enjoy. John McColgan had literally been the post-boy when I started as a radio announcer in Henry Street. He aspired to becoming a DJ and he took a great interest in the work of all the announcers. Brendan Balfe, John McColgan and myself became very friendly and, in time, John got himself on air, became a trainee in television and gradually worked his way up to becoming a producer/director. I liked his work and enjoyed his company immensely and so it seemed logical that I would ask him if he would be interested in directing the new series of *The Likes of Mike*. John readily agreed and we set to work.

John's was a most creative approach. He held onto the 'candid camera' elements of the previous series, reduced the song-and-dance content and added a 'Mike tries' slot, which involved my living out a number of my fantasies on television, such as sky diving, lion taming, scuba diving, an army assault course, horse-riding, and so on. The series was hugely successful and we followed it up with another one.

I had some narrow shaves during the course of making these programmes. I had always wanted to extend my self-knowledge to see just how much pressure I could withstand, on a physical and mental level, and this was my opportunity. I remember being scared stiff as I went into the lions' cage in Fossett's Circus in Bray. Two of the six lions had just had a fight and Nero, who was supposed to jump over my head, had had his nose badly bloodied. He was pretty disgruntled about the matter and was in extremely bad form. Before I went into the ring, the lion tamer, a rather large, well-scarred gentleman named Carl Fisher, had warned me that they were a little 'edgy this evening' and to take care not to fall because 'if they see you on the ground they'll jump on you'. I determined that my feet would at all times be firmly planted on terra firma.

When the show was broadcast, I did look somewhat tentative, even ashen-faced. When I entered the cage, Carl couldn't control the lions and they were running all over the place. Peter Dorney, the cameraman, actually followed me into the cage. He was incredibly courageous.

'I didn't really believe I was in there,' he told me afterwards. 'I had one eye closed and I kept thinking, I'm only watching television.'

Nero was supposed to climb up on a ramp and then, on my instructions, jump over my head and onto a ramp behind me. Nero did climb up on the ramp, alright. But he just stood there, snarling, eyes boring into me, blood dripping from his face. He also kept trying to swipe at me with his giant paw. All I could think of as I looked at him was 'Oh God, they look so much smaller at a distance.' He seemed gigantic up there, looking down at me. His head was huge. I kept banging my bamboo cane off the ramp, looking as stern as I possibly could and shouting 'Hup', as though I might lose my patience any moment and then Nero had better watch out! I think all I managed was a slightly petulant squeak!

Carl Fisher, meanwhile, was bellowing at Nero from behind, but this only served to confuse the animal. I plucked up courage and gave the ramp an almighty whack with my bamboo. This had the effect of startling Nero, who stopped, glared at me, snarled threateningly and then, grudgingly, jumped over my head and onto the far ramp. I was left with the legacy of a small drop of blood on my shirt shoulder. When I came out of the cage, I actually felt weak at the knees and John McColgan took me to a nearby pub for a whiskey. Instantly, I felt as if I was drunk. I don't recall ever being quite as scared of anything, before or since, although there were a few close contenders.

On one occasion, I permitted myself to be buried alive in Macroom. Tim Hayes, a small man from County Cork who was then the World Champion, having been buried for something like four weeks (I can't remember exactly how long), was on hand during the Macroom festival to offer me a few friendly words of advice before they lowered me into the ground.

'Don't get nervous, Mike,' were his words to me. 'Try not to let yourself get itchy, because you won't be able to sit up to scratch,' he added helpfully over the loudspeaker.

I was lowered six feet underground in the coffin, which had a small hole near my face through which was passed a one-inch-diameter pipe for air. The digger filled in the earth above me, so that I was completely entombed. People were permitted to have a few words with me as I lay in the coffin. One or two of them playfully covered up my airhole, which caused me no little concern, I can tell you.

After forty minutes, I felt I had had enough and wanted to come up. It was pretty claustrophobic down there and I was aware that, if I once lost my nerve, I would be a 'basket case' by the time they got me to the surface. It took them twenty-five minutes to remove all the earth and bring me out again. I decided then that the next time I went down in one of those things, it would be for real!

I also had a serious horse-riding accident. The intention was that I would ride in a 'bumper' race in the Phoenix Park, so I got to work, learning from scratch how to ride. I went to a riding school in Enniskerry and, of course, wanted to gallop immediately – *and* gallop like a jockey, standing up in the saddle.

Not unexpectedly, on about my sixth or seventh lesson, the horse ran away with me. It careered off towards the corner of the field with me holding on for dear life, pulling, straining and shouting for him to stop. To no avail. I knew what was going to happen before it happened. When the horse arrived at the corner of the field (which was walled) there was nowhere else for him to go, so he stopped dead in his tracks and, although I was trying to judge the moment when he would inevitably do so, I got it wrong. I was thrown over his head and landed extremely awkwardly on my head and hands. The upshot was that I was quite seriously concussed, needed eight stitches in my head and broke both my thumbs, one of them in four places. That took me a couple of months' recuperation. Undaunted, however, I carried on! I was determined to ride in that 'bumper'.

We contacted Mick O'Toole down at the Curragh and I left home every morning at six o'clock to ride out twice a morning with Mick's string of horses, jockeys and stable lads. He derived great amusement from the whole experiment. He'd roar at me as we were all circling the yard: 'Get your arse in the air, Murphy!' or 'Jasus, look at him, he's like Calamity Jane!' He was in his element. Naturally, he wouldn't let me ride any of his top racehorses, so he had me riding an old 'hack' of a thing, but I learned fast and eventually he used to permit me to go out on the gallops on the Curragh. I couldn't ride sitting down, I had only learned to ride standing in the stirrups like a jockey, but I simply loved the sensation of thundering up the gallops on one of those slim, nervous machines. It was one of the most exhilarating experiences of my life. I still regard riding racehorses at speed as one of my favourite 'highs'.

One morning, I was riding a bockety old mare out on the gallops in the middle of the Curragh. It was a beautiful morning and Mick had told me to be sure to keep the mare in her place in the order, during the gallop, and not to let her run away. What happened? You've guessed it! No sooner were were we up-and-going than the old thing decided that she could run faster than any of the stars of the stable who were ahead of her in the order. She took off on the outside, overtaking the other riders and horses, who were travelling in pairs at a pretty impressive canter. My charge, however, was at full gallop – and we weren't on the flat. She was gradually veering off into the rougher gorse and furze and I suspected I was going to have a major problem, because I simply couldn't stop her; I was just trying to hang on. Just when I thought I was going to be okay if I stayed in the saddle, her right foot went into a hole in the ground, she stumbled and, because I was in my usual precarious stance in the saddle, I promptly sailed through the air, landing with an almighty crash.

Mick came driving up in his car, hurling a few choice epithets at me that I hadn't heard before. The mare was caught and I hobbled up and was helped to remount her. Mick continued to berate me about my incompetence, lack of horsemanship, and so on. The stable lads, the jockeys, even the other horses, I think, were chortling to themselves with glee.

I was supposed to be going on to Cork to film something or other and John McColgan and the crew were to pick me up at Mick's place to drive me down. When they arrived, they heard the story, but I seemed to be okay so we headed off. They stopped in Kildare town so that I could have a large whiskey to help me get my wind back. When we reached Cashel, I wasn't feeling up to joining the others for lunch, so I stayed in the back of the car. By the time we continued our journey and were approaching Cork, I knew I was in trouble.

'You'd better get me to a hospital, I'm running out of breath,' I told them. I was also feeling a lot of pain in my chest.

They drove me to a nearby hospital, where I had to wait a while before being taken for an X-ray. Afterwards, we were left waiting again. The hospital seemed to be badly understaffed, nobody came back to me and nobody seemed unduly concerned.

'Come on,' I said. 'This is ridiculous. Let's let's get out of here. I'm feeling a bit better now.'

We left the hospital and, as we walked towards the cars, I had to grab onto a lamp post to help me regain my breath. Suddenly, there were shouts from behind us. It was a couple of orderlies with a stretcher who had been dispatched to drag me back for emergency surgery. The X-ray had shown that I had five broken ribs, that one of them had pierced my right lung, which had collapsed, and that my second lung was nearly gone, too.

The orderlies lay me down on the stretcher, but, in doing so, they cut off what remained of my air supply and I couldn't breathe at all. I grabbed the collar of one of them, but he thought that I was just nervous, not realising that I had stopped breathing and so couldn't speak. To stop me from strangling his companion, the other guy prevailed upon him to let me sit up.

I was brought inside to where a young doctor was standing by, looking quite nervous, I thought. He told me that, unfortunately, he was going to have to perform this small operation while I was conscious. So I sat there on the side of the stretcher while he opened my shirt and, with a scalpel and another sharp instrument, literally dug a small hole in my chest, into which he pushed a rubber hose. It was a pretty ghastly experience.

I had to stay in the hospital for ten days, while Eileen, Gran and the kids came down and had a relaxing sojourn in the comfort of a nearby hotel.

When I was released from hospital, I joined them at the hotel for a few days' recuperation. On the second afternoon, Eileen, myself and Deirdre, who was about three, walked slowly through the hotel grounds, which bordered the main Cork–Bandon road. Eileen and I walked ahead, while Deirdre played around us. I was very restricted in my movements, as I was still quite short of breath. When we reached the end of the garden, we both turned around to look for Deirdre – but she was missing. There were some gaps in the hedge and we both immediately panicked.

I ran down to and through the bushes and out towards the main road, but there was no sign of Deirdre. Then, as best I could, I tried to sprint back to the hotel, in the hope that she had gone back to the building. I was breathing in short gasps, while clutching my chest. I knew this was the worst possible thing I could do, but I couldn't help it as I was terrified that something had happened to Dee. There was a swimming pool near the hotel and I had to get there fast in case she had fallen in. When I reached it, the pool was empty and I ran upstairs to the hotel room – to find Deirdre sitting quietly playing with her toys.

A doctor was called and I was given a few whiffs of oxygen, and within an hour or so I was okay. But I can still remember the panic and the fear that I experienced over that incident.

I never did get to ride in that 'bumper' race, but we made a story of the accident for the TV programme. John insisted that they would have to re-enact the 'fall' for dramatic purposes, and they did – with a stuntman and a magnificent-looking racehorse! All for dramatic effect, of course!

Over the previous year or so, I was fortunate to have presented a fascinating television series, produced by one of Ireland's best film makers, David Shaw Smith. The programme was entitled *A World of Houses*, and its theme was Irish architecture from pre-history. It was a very rewarding series to be involved in and it was a pleasure working with a craftsman of the calibre of David and his wife Sally, who did sound, lighting, coffee – everything else, in fact. It was also a wonderful gateway to knowledge for me. I learned a great deal about history, architecture, social mores and traditions, as well as art, of course, from that series.

John McColgan and I had enjoyed working together so much that we resolved that, sometime in the next few years, we would make a major documentary series together. We were great friends and had tremendous respect for each other's work.

147

On a personal level, John was at that time going through a very painful marriage break-up. I recall one Christmas Eve when, after getting the bus to his family's home in Bray, County Wicklow (he couldn't afford a car at the time), laden with the children's Christmas presents, he simply left the presents in the porch and walked back down the long road to wait for the next bus to his mother's house, where he was staying.

Admittedly, I was only seeing the situation from one side, but to me he had always been a caring and loving father, and a generous man in every way. Those were tough times for John and he faced them with a great deal of courage and dignity.

John has since gone on to great things. He produced *The School Around the Corner* with Gerry Ryan, he directed the opening night of RTE 2 television, produced *The Dory Previn Show* and has made many other top-class shows for television. He is now quite a celebrity. He and his wife, Moya Doherty, whom he met when he was working in RTE 2 as Controller of Programmes, are the producers of the most successful stage show ever put on by an Irish company – *Riverdance*. It was typical of John and Moya that they would risk their all on producing the show. The fact that it has become such an incredible success is a tribute to their vision, tenacity and daring.

Since I wrote the above, they have been awarded the new National Radio Franchise. And no better people! It is rumoured that they are in the millionaire class now, and I hope such is the case.

The Fruits of Uncle Sam

In 1975, the United States Embassy in Dublin contacted me. Bob Jordan, who was the cultural attaché at the time, asked me if I would be interested in visiting the United States as a guest of the US government. Would I what?!

This was part of the US Visitors' Programme service, where journalists and people from the media were invited to visit the United States and record their impressions of it. Gay Byrne had already been invited, but apparently he had come home after a couple of weeks, even though one could stay for at least a month. Gay didn't seem to have enjoyed his visit very much, but I was very excited and couldn't wait to go.

You could either nominate the states or cities you wished to visit in the United States and it would all be organised for you, or you could simply decide to spend the entire four weeks in one place – Hawaii for example. Needless to say, I wanted to go everywhere! Eileen told me she felt exhausted even before we left at the thought of the schedule we had planned.

Sure enough, it proved to be a gruelling timetable. But exhilarating. I simply loved the place and couldn't see enough of it! At the end of the four weeks, we went to Mexico to visit Declan and he brought us out to the Yucatan Peninsula, where the Legion had one of their missions. This is a fascinating place, abounding in relics of the Mayan culture, the most impressive of which is the Great Pyramid of Chichén Itzá. I climbed to the top of the pyramid, despite the midday heat and thousands of scuttling iguanas. The area has since become one of the great tourist centres of the world, through its resort Cancun, which, when we were there, consisted of only one hotel.

In many of the places we visited, the US government had arranged that we would be feted by the mayor, or some local dignitary. We had gone to Mexico, prior to making our final official stop in the US in New Orleans and returning home via New York. We sent all our clothes ahead to New York from Mexico, before making our stop in New Orleans. However, I contracted a very severe dose of food poisoning in Mexico and was feeling none too well when we arrived in the steamy humidity of New Orleans.

It was with some dismay that I found, on arrival at the hotel, that we were invited to the mayor's office the next morning, where I was to be presented with the 'keys of the city'. Apart from not feeling well, I only had an old shirt, a pair of jeans and a corduroy jacket with me, and even Eileen was travelling in very casual clothes. Nonetheless, we tidied ourselves up as best we could and we went along to the mayor's office. He did look slightly askance, but mustered up enough old world courtesy to make a short speech and present me with a cardboard replica of the keys of the city of New Orleans.

That afternoon, we went to the tourist hotspot, Bourbon Street. I was too sick to do any walking and so lay down on the grass in the public park while Eileen went for a look around the shops. I fell asleep and was awakened by a black gentleman in a park attendant's uniform kicking me, none too gently, in the flank and telling me to 'get my ass out of there', that there was no sleeping allowed in the park. I protested along the lines of 'My good man, do you realise I have the freedom of the city?' but he wasn't overly impressed. He yanked me to my feet and pointed to the gate. Then he bent down behind me, picked up a nearly empty bottle of wine and shoved it into my hand, telling me to 'get the hell out' of the park and 'take my drink' with me. Eileen came round the corner at that moment to see me being bundled out of the park, protesting about the keys of the city and clutching my cheap bottle of wine.

I came back to Ireland all ready for action. I contacted John McColgan immediately.

'Okay,' I said. 'This is the idea. We're going to do a full series on America. I've made contacts, I know where we're going and I have a good idea of the outline of the programmes.'

John was enthusiastic. We went to see Dick Hill, who was then Head of Features and Documentaries at RTE.

'You two have no track record in anything as big as this,' Dick said. 'You've no experience in film making as such and you know you'll get no support from the people at the top. But,' he said, 'I've known you both for long enough to know how determined you are, and I'm going to give my full backing to the project.'

And he did. He backed us all the way. Even when we went over our budget and called him from a tiny motel room in Billings, Montana, telling him that we had run out of money, Dick reassured us and told us he'd handle it. He was tremendous.

John and I went to America for a ten-day 'recce' and came back more convinced than ever that there was 'one hell of a series' in this. We decided to break it down into six one-hour programmes: one in New York city, based on the New York police; one in Nashville, dealing with the country music phenomenon; Hollywood and the movies; Miami, tourism in Florida, the Everglades, old people on the beach; Las Vegas, gambling and entertainment; and Montana, the Western myth – cowboys and American Indians. We set off in 1977, John, myself, Ken Murphy on camera, Cedric Culleton as assistant camera, Brian Lynch to do sound and Mary Alleguen as production assistant. American Rob Adams, joined us as Road Manager in the US. And, however we managed it, we got some terrific television programmes.

The two weeks we spent with the New York police force opened our eyes to aspects of life that we hadn't even guessed at. We saw the seamy, dangerous side of police work. We came to understand why the police didn't wish to, literally, handle many of the vagrants they encountered in their everyday work, because, as one of them told us, 'They got diseases they don't even have names for yet.' They all felt the need to shower the minute they got home. Theirs was a dirty, unrewarding job.

In the main, they were good, brave people, but there were some appallingly twisted fascists and sadists among them. One night, an Irish cop boasted to us about how he liked to handcuff black suspects to an overhead pipe and beat them with his shoes, taking pride in doing it without leaving a mark. He was also expert at punching the kidneys, again without bruising.

Although most of their work was routine, there were moments of extreme tension and fear. We saw an elderly cop, sweating profusely, as we waited in the semi-darkness of a tenement building while his companion tried to flush out an intruder we knew was inside.

I got into a spot of bother with the so-called World Leader of the Hell's Angels. He was a big, grizzly giant of a man named Oden who, two weeks previously, had reputedly thrown a girl to her death from the roof of the Hell's Angels' building and then hightailed it on his motorbike to California. We were in a coffee shop with two plainclothes cops when, to their horror, Oden himself walked in. He was about six foot eight, nearly three hundred pound in weight, he had tattooed bare arms, a sheepskin waistcoat, spurs, chains and hair everywhere. Pretty impressive. He didn't speak, but just pointed at the coffee machine, leaned over the counter and grabbed a cream bun, and sat down noisily at a nearby table.

Despite the advice of the cops, I went up to him and tried to prevail upon him to do an interview. I emphasised the importance of doing an interview for Irish television, that the Irish people would appreciate the Hell's Angels philosophy, that we wouldn't keep him long anyway and that we would wait for him outside if he liked. He murmured 'go away' once or twice and 'beat it', before he eventually put down his cream cake, reached up, grabbed me by the collar and, with one hand, threw me across the shop and up against the counter, where I knocked over a stand of sandwiches. We left shortly after that, giving him a wide berth. I noticed that there was no move by our two 'protectors' to arrest the alleged murderer.

This time was pre-AIDS, and the cops educated us in the mores of the 'heavy' gay scene and the gay bars. We were informed about such unusual pastimes as 'fist-fucking', which is self-explanatory, and 'frog-fucking', which is so indelicate that I will refrain from describing the relevant details. Suffice it to say that the frogs were alive and kicking at the time.

We were in the precinct house that subsequently became known as 'Fort Apache', talking to the desk sergeant, a tough old 'buzzard' of a cop who had seen it all, when a small man in a Columbo-style raincoat walked past and said good evening to the sergeant. The sergeant pointedly ignored him and carried on talking to us. I asked him who the man was.

'That's the new lieutenant,' he said. 'He's down from Queens, but he ain't staying much longer. He's leaving.'

His attitude intrigued me, so I asked him why was the new lieutenant leaving so soon and he told us what had happened. The new lieutenant had arrived, determined to clean up the 'heavy' gay scene in his new precinct. He wanted to be taken around the gay bars to see just how bad the situation was, but nobody would volunteer to go with him.

'These guys are dangerous,' the sergeant explained. 'They get ya, they cosh ya to death. They carry knives. There's nothing sissy about these guys. They think you're a cop, you got a problem.'

Eventually, a sergeant even smaller than the lieutenant himself was delegated, despite his protestations, to accompany the lieutenant on his maiden voyage. The sergeant took him to the toughest bar first. There were men in Nazi helmets, Davy Crockett hats, cowboy outfits, there were weightlifters and truckdrivers, pretty muscular specimens, all either engaged in conversation or dancing together when the policemen arrived. The lieutenant looked around him, wide-eyed. They ordered a drink at the bar.

The sergeant said, 'Lieutenant, I got to go to the john. Anybody comes up and asks you to dance, you tell them you got a date, you're not dancing, okay?'

'Sure,' said the lieutenant.

The sergeant went to the toilet and, when he returned, found a very large, slightly drunk, truckdriver-type towering over the lieutenant, prevailing upon him to dance. The lieutenant was shaking his head, waving his hands and saying, 'No, I got a date, I got a date.'

The sergeant joined the twosome and said to the big guy, 'Hey, beat it! This is my date – go find your own.'

The big guy graciously enough said, 'Sorry, I didn't know. Have a good night!' and walked off.

'Hey, Lieutenant, you're not gonna like this,' said the sergeant, 'But you and me – we're gonna have to dance.'

So the lieutenant and the sergeant danced two numbers together, but while they were dancing they were spotted by an undercover cop who promptly reported back to his colleagues at the station house. From then on, the lieutenant was getting his reports signed 'Nightsick Charlie', 'Lovesick John' and so on, and was getting such a hard time from the Fort Apache boys that he had requested a transfer.

One night, we received a report that there was a 'jumper' in the vicinity. This was police jargon for a potential suicide. We hopped into our respective squad cars and hurried to the location. When we got there, the poor unfortunate man had already jumped. His body was covered by a sheet. A big Irish cop came over to us, all apologies.

'Jeez, guys,' he said, 'I'm really sorry. I said to him, "Hold it. There's an Irish TV crew in town. Could you wait till they get here?" But the bastard wouldn't wait. I'm really sorry, guys.' He was absolutely sincere. He had seen so much tragedy, sadness and drama that he was almost inured to everything but the social niceties of his obligations to the land of his fathers.

After this we moved on to Montana, where I rode a buffalo in a rodeo. Unfortunately, the damn thing threw me in such an awkward way that I landed on the buckle of my 'chaps' and was severely bruised, so much so that I had to be taken to a hospital. I spent the next couple of days on crutches.

Nashville was where I was to sing a song that had been composed for me in Dublin by Des Smyth. A good song it was too!

Well here I am in Nashville,
Singing in the Opry Show,
Singing and a-grinning,
Looking good for the women,
Hey, what a way to go!

We had already met such stars as Ray Stevens, Tammy Wynette, Don Williams, Tom T Hall and Waylon Jennings, and I had sought advice from all of them about how I should handle myself at the Grand Ole Opry and what pitfalls to watch out for. Don Williams was the one who put his feet on the table, laughed out loud and said, 'Well, just don't forget the words of the song!'

I was extremely nervous about my performance. We calculated that we could just about afford to pay for a group of four musicians to provide basic country music backing – nothing complicated. But the guys in question wouldn't even give me a practice run-through. Once they heard the tune, they nodded and said 'That's fine, we'll get it, we'll get it,' and left.

We didn't know at the time that, as soon as a television camera was present, the musicians' performance fee went up. So the word had gone out to every musician in town that there was an Irish TV crew around and that they'd be filming this evening, live at the Grand Ole Opry.

I was introduced by the legendary Roy Acuff. As I came out on stage, my introductory music commenced. I was stunned. It was too high, it was too fast and it sounded as though it was being played by the Berlin

Philharmonic Orchestra. Every musician in Nashville had decided to accompany me, as it meant an extra hundred dollars each for them. It was too late to do anything and I was too overcome with nerves to ask them to start again – lower and slower. I began to sing the song, trying to fit in with them, but doing so very badly.

I got through the first verse okay and then realised, with a horrendous surge of panic, that I couldn't remember the first line of the second verse. The orchestra kept strumming and thrumming along, while I trawled my brain. Eventually, in a conversational tone, I said to the audience, 'After twenty-five years of marriage, the husband turns around to the wife in bed and says, "I think I'll nibble your ear the way I used to." She says, "Don't be ridiculous. By the time you find your teeth, I'll be fast asleep." '

I told that 'joke' between the first and second verses of the song – it's there on television to prove it – and then I remembered the words of the second verse and began singing my way into legend. It was an experience I will never repeat. Nor will I be invited to, I hasten to add!

Hollywood was a difficult nut to crack. There was little novelty value for anyone in Hollywood in an Irish television crew trying to get interviews and seeking a small part in a major film. We got a few interviews with people like Rudy Vallee, the old crooner, who we interviewed in his magnificent home, high in the Hollywood Hills. He was a contrary old devil who, I gather, was something of a miser. He had a magnificent tennis court, but he liked to win; he would only play people he could beat. If they ever beat him, they were not invited back. After his death, it transpired that the tennis court itself was the roof of a huge room which contained all his treasures, and about which nobody knew. He told me that he and Bing Crosby were the two greatest singers of their generation, but that he had something extra.

'And what was the extra?' I asked him, innocently.

'I had a thing in my voice,' he said.

'What thing?' I asked.

'You know, *that* thing.'

I said I was sorry, but I didn't really know what he meant and would he explain.

Exasperated, he said, 'I was known as the guy with the "dick" in my voice.'

I nodded vigorously to show I had understood.

'Oh yes,' I said, 'Of course!'

We were also invited to film a photographic 'shoot' for *Hustler* magazine. The photographer was an Englishwoman named Suze Rendall. Suze was a former *Playboy* centrefold herself and had lived for a while in Hugh Hefner's mansion, but she was now one of the top photographers in the business. She was surrounded by a group of attractive young women she was 'shooting' for *Hustler*, and she was perfectly relaxed about our sitting in on the session.

It was a hilarious day. Ken, our cameraman, and Brian, our soundman, were almost traumatised by the goings-on in the studio. Young nubile women walked around in various stages of undress, often completely naked, and utterly oblivious to our presence. I was interviewing one of them, a naked black girl, while she was being made up by a young woman with long brown hair who, it transpired, was the younger sister of a very famous movie actress. The girl chatted with me as she was being made up. I noticed during the interview that the 'sister' had her bare foot on the chair between her subject's legs and was moving her toes. Needless to say, I didn't say anything. I was too busy trying to look as if I was attending mass at the time, or so Dick Hill told me afterwards when he saw the 'rushes'.

When the cameras had stopped rolling, I asked her, 'Did you intentionally have your foot where it was?'

'Oh yes,' she said, 'I was just giving Honey a "toe job". She likes that.'

It was later in the afternoon that one of the girls came over to Suze while she was talking to me and asked would it be okay if she took 'Mike' around the back to 'give him head'.

'Sure, no problem,' Suze said. 'Mike, you wanna go?'

I thought for a moment. A: had I understood the object of the request correctly, and B: was the Mike in question me?

It seems that I was correct on both counts, so I thanked the young woman very much for her consideration, said 'Oh God is that the time?' and told her that I was in a bit of a rush, but thank you very much anyway. I gather I looked a bit like a fish in a tank, with my jaws working and my eyes popping, as she shrugged her shoulders and walked away.

We still hadn't found a series or a movie for me to take part in – the size of the part didn't matter – the important thing was to gain access to the process of film making. We were near despair. It was Michael O'Herlihy, the Irish film director who was living in Hollywood, who eventually came to our rescue. We phoned Michael on the offchance and caught him in.

'Why don't you come up to my place and we'll chat about it?'

John and I called round and Michael agreed to give me a part as an extra in *The Man from Atlantis*, which he happened to be filming at the time.

Next morning, we took ourselves out to Malibu Beach, had a chat with Patrick Duffy (later to become Bobby in *Dallas*) and met some of the other stars of the series. Then Michael told me I was to be cast as a swimmer in an ocean race, as part of a group of twenty or so beach boys and athletes. I took a look at the other nineteen and knew I was at a grave disadvantage. They were all tanned, blonde and unbelievably muscular. I was lily-white, not so muscular and a pretty unimpressive swimmer at that. In fact, I didn't at all fancy the idea of going out of my depth in those big breakers. But, at the signal, we all raced into the raging surf – me and the beach boys. Having negotiated the breakers, with difficulty, I proceeded to attempt to do the crawl, like all the others. This was pretty difficult for me, as, at best, I usually manage a quite sedate breaststroke when I'm swimming. In no time, I was way behind the others, out of breath and floundering. But we had to do it again – and again.

158

I found out later that the first 'take' was perfectly okay, but that Michael O'Herlihy was so amused by the sight of, as he called it, 'this white-pelted Irishman tagging along behind the other swimmers, looking as if he could just as easily be drowning as swimming', that he had to do it again just for fun! I was knackered by the time filming was over and, not realising what a source of entertainment I had been, was quite surprised when, having staggered up to the pier from where O'Herlihy, his crew and my crew had been filming the action, they all burst into a spontaneous round of applause for my 'performance'.

It was while we were visiting Las Vegas that our Road Manager, Rob Adams, who was married to John's lovely sister Bridget, made a business suggestion to me that I have to say I regret I never followed up. Rob and Bridget were an incredible help to us in our trip around America, so much so that they had become essential members of the team. Rob spoke about the growing fashion in America for video shops and said that, since I was making *Murphy's Golden Movies*, as my 'candid camera' endeavours were called at the time in Ireland, that I should open a video shop under that name when I went home. Both John and myself thought it was a very good idea, as we had noticed this new trend in America of hiring video recorders and tapes, but we never got around to it. Today, both John and I regret that we didn't take Rob's advice and do what he suggested.

In Las Vegas we experienced the wacky and wonderful world of gambling and entertainment. We visited Elvis Presley's suite in the Hilton Hotel and unwittingly disturbed a celebrated black entertainer who was himself entertaining an attractive young woman in the principal bedroom when we walked in. He was pretty nonchalant about it and told us not to worry, to carry on looking around and that, if it was okay with us, he'd carry on with what he was doing!

We got the guided tour of Caesar's Palace, met Shirley MacLaine, who put on a superb stage show, Bob Hope, Peter Ustinov, Paul Anka, Wayne Newton, Michael Douglas, and many other stars. It was a fascinating glimpse behind the scenes at this incredible world of glamour and, it must be said, corruption. Money changed hands at every level. The more money that changed hands, the greater the welcome. Not with the stars, I hasten to add, but with many others.

We were lucky to have as our guide and host Joe Delaney, a gentleman of Irish extraction who had made his home in Vegas and had quite a reputation as a showbiz columnist. Joe was decent, courteous, well-liked and had easy access to anything and everyone in Las Vegas.

We also met Brendan Bowyer there, and he told me the story of one of the dancers from the first series of *The Likes of Mike*. Rita was small, red-headed and very funny, with a pronounced Dublin accent, and I liked her immensely. She had gone to Las Vegas with Brendan and the Big Eight as one of the dancing troupe. One night, Elvis Presley invited them all to his suite in the Hilton and, of course, they were only too thrilled to attend. The drink and the food were lavish – and it was all free.

While Brendan was engaged in conversation with Elvis, Rita went up to the bar and loaded up with glasses and bottles of booze. As she returned, she passed Brendan, who was telling Elvis what a great actor he was.

'I ain't a great actor,' Elvis was protesting. 'I'm a good singer, but I ain't a good actor. I can't act at all. In fact, I'm just a singer who does some acting, that's about it.'

Rita, laden with drinks, stopped and interrupted the conversation.

'Listen Elvis, d'ye know what your problem is?' she said, in her broad Dublin accent.

'I beg your pardon, ma'am?' he said.

'D'ya know what's wrong with you, Elvis?'

'What ma'am?'

'You underestimate yourself, Elvis, that's what's wrong with you. You'll have to get a bit more confidence!' and she walked off. Apparently, Elvis derived great amusement from the exchange.

It was in Las Vegas that Cedric and I spent an entire night at a blackjack table. There were no windows so we didn't see the next day dawn, but by morning we had lost about a hundred dollars each, which was pretty steep considering how close to being broke we were. Ken Murphy arrived.

'Come on, it's half past eight,' he said, 'We're filming in half an hour. I suppose you've both lost money?'

Ken would never gamble. In fact he was a very conservative man who was occasionally quite shocked by the behaviour of the rest of us.

'I think you're mad, spending the night gambling like that,' he said, and frankly we were forced to agree, especially in the circumstances.

'I wouldn't gamble if it was my last dollar,' he said, and turned and left.

Moments later, we heard sirens and whistles as a lucky gambler scooped one of the big machine jackpots. Cedric and I left the blackjack table and went over to see the excitement. To our utter disgust, we discovered that, as he was passing the big machine, Ken had put in a silver dollar, pulled the handle and hit the jackpot. He had won a thousand silver dollars! He could hardly contain himself, he was so excited.

Part of his prize was a huge and very attractive cuddly toy coyote, which was about three to four feet in length. We were returning home to Ireland within the next day or two and Ken was determined to bring the coyote with him. On the Aer Lingus flight from New York, Cedric and I were sitting together, the coyote was in an overhead compartment and Ken was four or five rows ahead of us.

I knew one of the air hostesses and asked her if she would help me 'set up' poor old Ken. She went and spoke to him and we could see Ken snap out of his reverie. She went on up the plane and Ken came rushing back to us.

'You're not going to believe this,' he said, 'but the FBI have called the plane. They suspect that someone is carrying drugs in a toy coyote.'

'That's nonsense!' I replied. 'Don't worry about it, Ken. It's not you, so you've nothing to worry about.'

Ken went back to his seat, slightly mollified. Later, one of the flight deck crew was walking past and Ken attracted his attention.

'Yes, sir?'

'Captain, excuse me,' said Ken. 'About the drugs in the coyote? Well, that's me.'

The Captain smiled and said, 'Oh yes. Well, have a nice flight, sir,' and moved on.

When we got to Shannon, we had the usual early-morning stopover before flying on to Dublin and, as we sat over coffee in the Departure Lounge, Cedric suggested we might take the prank a little further. So, I found two Customs men and told them the story and asked if they would help. They agreed, and went to Ken and asked him to accompany them to the plane, as they wanted to check out his coyote. Ken looked around for me and asked me to come with him, so we all went back to the plane. Ken went to get the coyote from the overhead locker.

'Hold it there, sir,' said one of the men, 'Let me do that.'

He reached up, took down Ken's coyote and took a penknife from his pocket.

'I really don't think you should worry, gentlemen,' I said, 'I can vouch for this man. There is no question that he has drugs in this coyote.'

'Are you quite sure, Mr Murphy?'

'Yes, you can trust me; I'm on television.'

'Well alright, so, Mr Murphy,' they said.

We all went back to the lounge bar, but it had gone a bit too far by now and Ken was truly rattled. It was one of those japes that had seemed like a good idea at the time but had got out of control, and now there was no going back. Ken was in quite a state and proceeded to tell the rest of the crew what had happened, although of course they already knew.

Neither Cedric nor myself could find it in our hearts to tell him that it was all a joke, for fear of his reaction. And it wasn't until something like three years later that Ken caught me outside the canteen and pushed me up against the wall.

'You rat!' he said. 'I've only just found out it was you that pulled that stroke on me about the coyote.' He took it in good part, however, even though he found, as he was telling the story to his colleagues in RTE, that they had already heard about it from the other side!

We were in America for two eight-week periods and, when we returned, John and editor Pat Duffner got to work on the post-production. They did a superb job. John and I wrote the script and we were very proud of the finished product when it was transmitted. *Murphy's America* was widely acclaimed and was to win me the first of four Jacob's Awards. The other ones, incidentally, being for *The Live Mike*, *Murphy's Australia*, and *Morning Call* on radio.

Up in the Mawnin', out on the Air

Dick Hill was appointed Controller of Programmes for RTE 2 and was to oversee the opening and administration of the new channel. The opening night was held in the Cork Opera House. John McColgan directed and I was compère for the evening. I recall that the musical introduction, which consisted of song, dance, and orchestral interludes and was originated by John, was received by some with rapture and by others with misgivings as being altogether too modern, too popular, too lowbrow. I am reminded of this when I think of what John was ultimately to do, so successfully, with the *Riverdance* show.

Many people were looking forward to the repartee that was anticipated between Terry Wogan, who was guesting, and me, as compère. I had by that time gained a reputation for wisecracking on radio, and Wogan was already a major institution on early-morning radio in Britain. Some people thought, quite wrongly, that there was some rivalry between us, possibly because there was a certain similarity in our styles. On the night, he and I had a brief chat before we went on stage, and then went on and engaged in a few minutes of banter. The general consensus seemed to be that it was quite entertaining and it was more or less declared a draw. (Curiously, when I have worked in Britain, I have often been referred to as an 'Irish Terry Wogan'.) One way or another, it was a very successful opening to the second national television channel.

When I returned from America, RTE radio asked me to take over the early-morning radio slot, *Morning Call*. This decision needed a great deal of thought, because it would necessitate my going to bed by ten and rising at five-thirty. My children were at the stage where they needed more of my time and attention rather than less, and if I were to change my lifestyle in this way I knew it would put further limitations upon my time with them. Eileen and I discussed it and we both agreed that, from a career point of view, it was something I should do. Eileen said she would handle things at home as best she could, and I promised to make myself as available as possible. I was also aware that I would have major television commitments to cope with during the daytime as well.

Up until then, *Morning Call* had been a pleasant enough, if harmless, programme. I recall how, one day some years earlier, Kevin Roche, who was Head of Music at the time, had called me into his office and asked if I had heard Aidan O'Hara's presentation of *Morning Call*. I said that I had.

'Well,' he said, 'That's the way to broadcast an early-morning programme.'

In truth, I had always found Aidan's style of broadcasting quite bland, and I said so to Kevin. However, Kevin Roche had since been succeeded by Billy Wall, who had also created *The Gay Byrne Show* when RTE extended its times of broadcasting from ten until one. Billy gave me a free rein and teamed me up with producer Gene Martin.

Gene was, over the course of the next seven years, to become one of my greatest friends. I had known him since the days when I had worked with Peter Hunt and Morgan O'Sullivan on the *Gael Linn Newsreel* soundtracks in Peter Hunt's studio. Even then, 'Geno', as he was known, was a true original. Grey-haired, dapper and always beautifully turned out, he favoured a bow tie and had a penchant for wearing odd socks. He had a wonderful turn of phrase and could be exceedingly, if entertainingly, disparaging about those of whom he disapproved. He loved antiques, paintings, sculpture, music, good architecture, wine and whiskey and was very much a 'social animal'. He was also blessed with an irreverent streak of mischief, which I was only too happy to encourage, and we embarked on *Morning Call* with glee.

In the early days of the programme, the county council workers on the Ennis Road objected to something I had said about them 'leaning on their shovels'. What I had actually said was that, when driving past, I had spotted them 'breastfeeding their shovels'. The County Manager formally objected on their behalf, so naturally they became a long-term target. We had awful Irish showband recordings of the time, and these, along with pompous politicians, irregularities in State bodies and the like, all became grist to our mill. Gene also liked nothing better than to 'send up' the weathermen. He had a little cassette of sneezes and belches and, when the weather report was being presented, he would wait for a pause and then activate the cassette machine. People would occasionally mention it, but were probably not too sure whether they had heard the belch on the radio or whether somebody in their own company had behaved in this vulgar fashion so early in the morning. We also took great delight in playing the rousing 'Erica' march from the Panzer Grenadiers at unearthly hours to waken the populace, despite the fact that there were one or two objections because it was said to arouse memories of Nazi Germany.

Over the next few years, *Morning Call* became the most popular programme on Radio 1. At one stage we had thirty-five per cent of the total listenership, which was twelve per cent more than *The Gay Byrne Show*. For Geno and myself, despite the inconvenience of the hours, it was great fun.

In those early days of *Morning Call*, Gene and I would often head down to the Magnet Pub in Pearce Street at nine o'clock in the morning, after the programme. We would have two hot whiskeys and cheese and tomato sandwiches and then, if I was free, we would visit the galleries and the auction rooms.

On these trips I learned a great deal about painting and sculpture from Gene, who had strong views about design, colour, furniture, glass – everything visual, in fact. He also had a fascination with birds. He could distinguish house martens from swallows at a distance. He would stand for long minutes, watching a pair of magpies arguing on the grass. In fact, some years later, after he had crashed his car into a lamppost, he admitted to me that he had been watching a couple of seagulls bickering when it happened.

Marian Finucane told me recently that, when giving lectures, she often speaks about the importance of the producer/presenter relationship, and she always quotes Gene Martin and myself as the best such combination she has encountered. Marian would occasionally stand in for me on *Morning Call*, but she confessed that she was never truly comfortable in the niche. *Liveline*, however, was just around the corner for her.

After three years, the early mornings and the strain on our home life was proving too much for me and I requested a change. RTE agreed and moved me to a lunchtime slot. I think it was Valerie McGovern who took over from me on *Morning Call*.

It was during the run of this lunchtime programme that an unfortunate incident occurred between Ulick O'Connor and myself. Ulick was a regular contributor to the programme, as indeed he had been to many other programmes with which I had been involved. I enjoyed Ulick's incisive mind and was quite capable of handling his occasional abrasiveness. He had written an excellent biography of Oliver St John Gogarty, and his book *Celtic Twilight* is probably the best book written about the Gaelic Literary Revival.

Ulick appeared on the Sunday midday programme (which didn't involve me) and talked on the subject which he was scheduled to speak about on our programme the following Wednesday. My producer, Maura Clarke, took what was, in my view, the correct decision and cancelled his appearance on Wednesday, on the basis that he had already spoken on the air about that subject. Ulick was incensed, so much so that he took legal action against RTE. I kept reassuring Maura, Adavin O'Driscoll (the then Head of Light Entertainment), Colin Morrison and all the other producers that it would never get to court, that Ulick would pull out because he hadn't a leg to stand on. However, a date was set for the lawsuit. Again, I confidently reassured my colleagues that there was nothing for them to worry about.

To my surprise, the day before the court date I received a phone call from a firm of solicitors informing me that I had been subpoenaed to appear. I explained that I was engaged the following day and would not be in a position to turn up, but they told me that I was legally bound to be present. I agreed to be there at 2 o'clock, which was the scheduled time for the hearing, but that I would have to leave at 2.15 sharp, and they guaranteed that I would be the first witness.

It was almost 2 o'clock when I arrived at the courtroom. I went over to my radio colleagues and told them that there was no need to worry and that it would be sorted out to our satisfaction. I saw Ulick and his people standing over to one side and gave them a cursory nod.

The judge took his seat and called me as the first witness. I was asked had I worked with Ulick before, to which the answer was in the affirmative, did I think he was a good broadcaster, to which I answered again in the affirmative and, finally, did I think he had been treated fairly on this occasion. I was quite expansive in my response. I said that not alone did I think he had been treated fairly but that I was totally in agreement with the producer's decision; that Ulick had had an extraordinary amount of public exposure during the course of my programmes and that, as far as I was concerned, it was a waste of everybody's time his taking this case. There were no further questions and I was told that I could step down. I left, waving cheerfully to my colleagues. Around five o'clock that evening, I phoned RTE to find out how the case had gone. Colin Morrison told me that Ulick's case had been dismissed. I was quite taken aback.

'Why was that?' I asked.

'The judge said there was no contract. And, by the way, there was a lot of reaction to your appearance. Apparently, you had been subpoenaed to appear on *their* behalf, but you effectively destroyed their case in the first few minutes.'

Ulick and I have never spoken about the matter since, but relations have been somewhat strained.

In 1985, I was invited by Concern, the Third World Organisation, to visit Bangladesh and India as part of their media campaign in which they encourage journalists, and radio and TV people generally, to come and see their work. I decided that it would be a good opportunity to pass on my mother's precepts to the next generation and that I would invite one of my daughters to go with me. Elaine, who was seventeen at the time, wasn't too keen, so I approached Carol, who was next in line. I had some misgivings about bringing a sixteen-year-old to the Third World, where she would be exposed to some pretty traumatic sights, but Carol was very outgoing and imbued with a great sense of adventure, so I felt that she would be able to cope.

We spent three weeks touring Bangladesh and then went to Calcutta, in India. Both of us were shocked by what we saw and we soon realised that poverty as we knew it in Ireland bore no comparison whatsoever to the poverty of these people. We saw open drains running down the middle of the streets; dead babies caught in the reeds at the bend of a river (when a mother was unable to take care of her baby, she would drown it and release its body into the flow of the river); the women tea-gatherers of the north who were forced into prostitution in the factory camps; the indescribable smell of disease, deprivation and death. I wrote a series of articles for the *Sunday Press* in which I tried to capture my reactions to what I saw.

Carol was profoundly affected by Bangladesh. She has a strong maternal instinct and, within a few days, volunteered to take charge of the babies in some of the camps we visited. She amazed me with her remarkable maturity and adaptability.

When we arrived in Calcutta, we were almost overcome by the sheer volume of people. The city is so over-populated that there is almost nowhere you can walk without encountering people standing, sitting or lying on the pavement. Families literally live on the pavement. They have an area about twelve feet by five, against the railings, which is their home. They have a tarpaulin tied to the railings which they pull down over them at night. They have their pots and pans, they light fires, they are born, they live and they die on that small area of pavement. Apparently, they also pay 'protection' money to a Mafia-style gang for the privilege of this existence.

We stayed in a hotel in the centre of the city with Father Jack Finucane of Concern. Each time we walked out into the street, we were immediately accosted by at least twenty beggars, many of them physically mutilated, some of them on makeshift wheels as they had no legs, all of them tugging at our clothes and trying to catch our gaze. It is impossible to help them all and the only way to deal with it is not to make eye contact with any one of them. If you do, that person will follow you everywhere, if you are on foot. And if you give them alms, he or she tells the others and you are inundated by yet another shouting, mauling crowd.

On our second day, Carol informed Jack and myself that she was going shopping. We said that we would accompany her, but she was determined to go alone. I was desperately nervous, permitting her to go out in those streets, where the law is almost non-existent and anything could happen to a young and unchaperoned foreign girl, but I could not dissuade her. She pointed out to me that I had always wanted my children to express themselves, to have a sense of adventure and to show no fear, and so it was impossible to stop her. She was gone for over two hours. Jack kept reassuring me that she was extremely capable and strong-willed, and that she would be fine, but I was very worried and feared that I had been irresponsible. I knew I could not tell Eileen that I had let Carol go out alone into that mêlée. However, she eventually returned. Not alone did she return, but she had with her a native porter carrying her goods – 'Number 57', she called him. She had had a wonderful time, had done all her shopping and had engaged Number 57 for a small fee to be her porter. I was both relieved to see her and proud of her independence of spirit.

I am in the very fortunate position of being able to admire all of my children. Elaine is an inordinately gifted young woman, artistically. She is currently working in ceramics and has spent five years living in the United States. I have seen Elaine suffer setbacks, injuries and pain, and she has never flinched. I have never once seen her physically afraid in any situation – something I greatly admire in her. Deirdre, our third daughter, is the same. She is self-sufficient, probably the most independent of them all, and great fun to be with. Mark, the youngest, is now eighteen years of age and, like Deirdre, is working in the music business. He is a self-contained, confident young man who is sure of himself and his place in the world and yet, like my other children, is compassionate and sensitive to other people's needs.

I have always maintained that I would prefer my children to like me rather than love me (although I do want them to love me too, if the truth were known). There is an element of duty when it comes to children loving their parents, but I would hope for more. The fact that they like my company, enjoy conversing with me, want to share their life experiences with me is far more important to me.

After about eighteen months on the lunchtime slot, RTE asked me to revert to *Morning Call*, as they had decided to extend the hours from seven-thirty until ten o'clock, right up to Gay's time, and they would like me to do a major interview during the nine-fifteen to ten slot. Again, I thought about it for a long time and, warming to the challenge of the interview every morning, I finally accepted. So, it was business as usual with Gene for a further three years.

During that time I interviewed almost every prominent person in the country: politicians, sportspeople, members of the religious community, topical newsmakers, musicians, composers, movie stars. It was a difficult brief, because I had very little time in which to do any research. They were also long interviews, approximately forty minutes in length, and 'live'. But the series was very successful, and has proved to be a valuable source of archive material.

At this remove, it is difficult to recall the more memorable interviews. I interviewed major politicians of the day such as Charlie Haughey, Jack Lynch, Garret FitzGerald, an up-and-coming Kerry politician named Dick Spring, and many others. There were people from the world of sport, like Tony Jacklin, Christy O'Connor, Steve Davis – and Alex Higgins, who distinguished himself by not turning up! I should have known better with Alex, as, a year or so previously when I was taping an interview with him for the TV programme *The Live Mike*, he had asked me, during the interview, how much he was to be paid. When I told him that it would be two hundred pounds, he stated that Eamonn Andrews paid double that amount and that he wouldn't cross the road for 'that kind of buttons'. He then stomped out, leaving us with a four-minute, unfinished TV interview. There was also Kadar Asmal, Faye Dunaway – for whom we threw a lavish lunch in one of the small radio boardrooms, much to the astonishment of the Controller in the next room – Spike Milligan, Shirley Conran, and many more.

Some of the interviews do stand out in my memory. I vividly recall the interview I did with the Reverend Ian Paisley in our Belfast studio. It was at the height of the Troubles and we were quite surprised that Paisley had agreed to the interview. It was not pre-announced for security reasons, and I turned up at the RTE studio in Belfast on the appointed morning. I completed the *Morning Call* section of the programme from seven-thirty until nine and then Paisley arrived. The security was very intensive. There were armed men posted on the roof and outside every door, and Paisley himself arrived with a group of his own security people. He entered the studio – bluff, jolly, no-nonsense.

'What's this all about? How do I find myself talking to a Southerner? And you're probably a Catholic at that!' he thundered, as he amiably shook my hand.

We sat down and did a very agreeable interview. It wasn't soft, either – there were some hard questions, leading to a few spirited exchanges. At about ten minutes to ten he said, live on air, 'Well, I have to leave you now. I have to go to a church service.'

'Could you not just hang on for another few minutes?' I asked.

'No, no. I must go,' he replied, 'My people await me and I have a major collection to take up.'

'A silent one, of course,' I said.

'Of *course*,' he agreed, and wished me farewell. He had no sooner gone out of the door than he came back with a photographer in tow.

'I'd like to have my photo taken with you. Would you let me stand beside you for a moment?' And this we did, while a record played.

For me, however, the humour of the situation ended dramatically, immediately after the programme, when a police superintendent asked if he could have a word with me. He told me that during the course of the programme the police had received a threat on my life, or on the life of a member of my family. They were taking the threat seriously, because the correct password of the day had been given. He said that I would be escorted to the border by the RUC, where I would be met by the gardaí with an armed escort. I was naturally frightened for the safety of Eileen and the children, but he told me that the police were already outside the house and that they had checked my children's classrooms and were keeping the school under observation.

The drive home from Belfast that day was my longest ever. The idea that Eileen or the children might be in mortal danger was unthinkable. I blamed myself for agreeing to interview a man who was regarded by some as a religious bigot. If anything had happened to my children or to Eileen, I don't believe I would ever have forgiven myself. As it happened, the gardaí kept up their surveillance for the next week or so and gradually the threat just faded away.

Eamon Dunphy was an interesting interviewee. I recall opening the interview with Eamon by saying, 'I have just read your book, *Only a Game*, and, had I been a member of the Millwall squad at the time you were there, I would have been queuing up to punch you, because of your lack of application, your niggardliness and your general negative demeanour.' I had used such an opening on the basis that Eamon was no slouch himself in terms of dishing it out and so I expected that he would be fairly sanguine about such an approach. But this was not the case. After the programme, Eamon complained that I had abused my position as a broadcaster. I remember this with some irony when I read the unkind and often insulting things Eamon sometimes writes about others.

My interview with Cristabel Bielenberg precipitated her book and the TV series of her life. I recall how, during the course of the interview, she sat opposite me with her head slightly averted from the microphone and spoke in a slow, unemotional, almost detached way about her awful experiences in Nazi Germany. It was one of the most moving interviews I have ever done.

The Mike Goes Live

RTE 2 television was now in full swing, under the guiding hands of Dick Hill, Ted Dolan and John McColgan. Muiris MacConghail, who was Controller of Programmes in RTE 1, asked me if I would present a regular Friday night show on his channel. *The Late Late Show* was successfully capturing the multi-channel audience on Saturday nights and the RTE Authority was looking for a programme which would do the same on Friday nights. He told me that John Keogh, who was now working for television, would be the producer and we could put together our own team and have more or less whatever facilities we liked, as long as the format was interesting. Basically, we could please ourselves, as long we won the Friday night ratings for RTE 1.

John Keogh and I met and decided that we would base the new show on a mythical evening in company. If one analyses an enjoyable social gathering, its success is never solely due to jokes or anecdotes or laughter. In terms of conversation, the most satisfying occasions invariably turn out to be those that have included good humour, a degree of satire, or bitchiness, if you like, and a substantially serious element. This was what we decided to use as the model for *The Live Mike*. We decided that, yes, we would have comedy, yes, we would have entertainment, but that we would also, irrespective of any criticism, stop everything to include a serious piece of journalism or investigative reportage in the middle of the programme.

We put together a wonderful team. There was David Blake Knox, who was a new young director, just out of training, for whom both John and I had a great deal of respect. Joe McCormick was assigned to us as director. Joe was an old hand – grey-haired, genial, American-trained. He had been a bandleader and a movie actor in his day and was relaxed, funny and all set to enjoy this new lease of life. Larry Masterson – stocky, bearded, a Dubliner and proud of it – had been one of the founder members of the Simon Community as well as a newspaper journalist. He was the kingpin of our research team, one of the new breed of researcher in RTE, determined to get right to the heart of a matter, pursuing stories where others didn't wish to go, hard-nosed and yet a deeply sensitive man. Years later, Larry was to become my business partner. At the suggestion of Eoghan Harris, I asked Muiris to recruit Kevin Linehan, who at that time was working with the Revenue Commissioners and who had expressed an interest in becoming a researcher with RTE. Shay Howell, who was a good friend of ours, was also brought in as a researcher.

So here we were, with as lively and interesting a backroom team as anyone could imagine.

The front-of-house members of our team almost chose themselves. Dermot Morgan had been writing for me on morning radio for a number of months and I really enjoyed his scripts. John Keogh had seen Dermot perform at a university 'bash' and liked his style, so Dermot was taken on. Twink had not yet been properly exploited in terms of television, but I realised that, with her talent for comedy, she could be a major hit. So Twink was approached and was delighted to be involved. We needed one extra person with a flair for comedy, who would also be able do a bit of acting and some scriptwriting, and so Fran Dempsey was contracted. Then there was Tony Boland, who was to look after the booking of musicians and the special guest slot. So here we had a truly top-class team of people, all of whom were looking forward to this new challenge, and prepared to enjoy it in the process.

We set to work with great optimism and enthusiasm. We knew there were many political targets out there for the 'plucking', we were certain the 'candid camera' section would be a success, as it had been on previous programmes, and we felt that we were well equipped musically. We were confident that Twink's impersonations, Dermot Morgan's character creations, as well as Fran's rubber features would guarantee that the programme was a comedic success. The only uncertainty we had was about the middle, or sociological, section, which was the biggest gamble.

We went live with our first programme in November 1979 and, immediately after transmission, I was called to studio reception for a phone call. It was Muiris, who told me that he had watched it at home and believed that it would be *the* big winner of his tenure as Controller. He congratulated the entire team and said that he thought that the central piece, which featured a man who was illiterate and whose boss didn't know, had fitted in very well with the rest of the programme. He congratulated us on our nerve in incorporating it into the format and hoped we would enjoy the success that was going to come our way.

And successful *The Live Mike* was. It continued for three years. Dermot Morgan emerged from it as a top-class performer and writer, Twink created a career from it and I received another Jacob's Award. David Blake Knox is currently RTE's Assistant Director of Television, Kevin Linehan is Head of Young People's Programmes, Larry Masterson, is probably the foremost independent TV producer in the country, and Shay Howell is a highly respected senior researcher in RTE. Joe McCormick moved to Galway 'to go fishing', as he said himself, and comes back occasionally to direct programmes for RTE, and Tony Boland is one of the owners of Planet Television, which created *The Big Breakfast* for Channel 4. John Keogh continued his musical career with

Full Circle and is still producing programmes, as well as appearing on TV in such offerings as *The Lyrics Board*.

The Live Mike team shared a variety of interests and talents. I was interested in art and I was dabbling in buying and selling paintings, Shay Howell was an avid book collector and occasional dealer, and we all had an interest in stocks and shares. So, no day would pass without either books or paintings being sold or exchanged, or share prices being discussed and, in many instances, acted upon. We had a couple of accounts with stockbrokers and we played the stock market, not unsuccessfully, for about a year and a half.

From the beginning there was a decided rivalry between *The Late Late Show* and *The Live Mike*. *The Late Late Show* was riding high in the ratings, always at number one and invariably totally unchallenged. Our very first programme leapfrogged over *The Late Late Show* and shot straight to the number one spot. This was dramatic news throughout the station and was a source of tremendous relish to our little band. Our annexe – annexe five – backed on to *The Late Late Show*'s annexe and my group immediately hung banners from our windows with 'Number One' scrawled across them. Somewhat childish, in retrospect, and regarded with tight-lipped disapproval by *The Late Late Show* team, who, in fact, were quite disapproving in general of the antics of *The Live Mike* team. Gay, as producer, ran a very tight ship in *The Late Late Show* office: people were expected to be in on time, to notify Gay if they left the office, to explain why they might be late back after lunch and generally to disport themselves in a manner that would befit a highly efficient insurance company office. I have often teased Gay about his penchant for efficiency, punctiliousness and general Good Sense. One day we were presented with the opportunity to play what we considered to be a wonderful prank on Gay – and we could not resist.

A gentleman named Des McCarthy, who was a pretty unconventional character from Limerick, arrived in our annexe with a big wooden box about four feet by two and deposited it on the floor. There was chicken wire on the top and a section of the box was blocked off. Through the chicken wire we could see remnants of apples and cabbage stumps, and bits of half-eaten potato. A furry tail was visible, but we were unable to see the body of the animal that owned it. Des told us that what he had in the box was a mongoose, and that it would be terrific entertainment for the audience on *The Live Mike*. He said that the mongoose was asleep at the moment but that he would wake it up with a stick and then we would see what would happen. He told us that we were in no danger, that the chicken wire was very strong and the mongoose couldn't get out, but that, if it did, it would go straight for our ankles and its jaws were so strong that it would actually be able to crush the bone.

The entire team had by now gathered around the box to see what would happen and Noel Green, one of the Light Entertainment producers, had also come in to have a peep. Des began to make noises and rattle around the animal's leisure area with the stick. The tail did not move. Then he began to prod the tail itself, all the while telling us 'You'll see him now, he'll come running out. He'll be spittin' and makin' noises and hissing at you, but he can't get out, you needn't worry.'

Next minute he brought the stick up to near the top of the chicken wire and, as he did so, the catch lifted and suddenly the 'creature' flew through the air and landed on Noel Green's knee. Noel screeched and ran for the door. As he did, we saw that it was only a piece of fur and that the whole thing had been a practical joke.

I don't know who suggested it, but somebody said, 'Wouldn't it be a terrific idea to try that out on Gay?' The idea greatly appealed to me and so we went over to Gay, who was in his office with one or two members of his staff. I introduced Des, who came in carrying the box.

'Listen,' I said to Gay. 'This is a terrific programme idea. We're not going to be able to use it on Friday night, but it might come in handy for you on Saturday. Just let me show it to you.'

He came from behind his desk and leaned back against it with his legs crossed in front of him. I positioned the box so that what was about to happen would be as spectacular as possible. Des explained that the mongoose was a vicious little thing, that it would bite right into your bones, that it would spit but not to worry, and so on. Then he began to fiddle around inside the cage with the stick. By now I could see that the window was almost blocked with the heads of my colleagues, waiting for their 'moment in a million'. I told Gay he would really enjoy this, that it was 'terrific entertainment', while Des continued to poke around with the stick.

'Des,' I said, 'Give it a good hard bang. See if you can make it come out.'

Des lifted the stick, flipped the catch and out flew the 'creature'. It landed precisely where I had intended – right on Gay's ankles. He let a out yell, turned and ran back towards the wall, where there was a filing cabinet, and proceeded to try and climb up the handles of the drawers. By this stage, the members of *The Live Mike* team were banging their approval at the window and Gay realised he had been 'had'. Like the good sport that he is, he took it extremely well, but asked me 'please, not to bring any more programme suggestions over to the office'.

During the course of *The Live Mike* series, we frequently broke new television ground. We followed a man who was going to have a vasectomy, spoke with a lesbian about prejudice, sex, family and so on, and interviewed a young woman who was a prostitute and who told us some very dark and disturbing things about her life. Dolores Lynch was her name and we filmed her in silhouette. In the course of the interview she spoke about the savage beatings she received from her husband and said that her life was in danger because she had refused to co-operate with him. About four years later, Kevin Linehan came into my office – Kevin was by this stage working with the current affairs programme *Today, Tonight* – and asked me if I had a tape of the interview with Dolores. I told him I had not, but that I was sure that it was in the library.

'Dolores was murdered last night,' he said, 'and the tape has mysteriously disappeared from the library.'

Apparently Dolores' house was set fire to while she was asleep, and the police believed it to be murder. We don't know where the tape went. It was never traced and, to this day, some people think that it was deliberately removed from the library.

It was also during *The Live Mike* years that I lost my appetite for the 'candid camera' part of the show. It had been a remarkably successful element of both *The Likes of Mike* and *The Live Mike* and, even today, people still comment on the pleasure it gave them. The best remembered one is the time I caught out Gay Byrne in Trinity College.

We had gone to elaborate lengths to set Gay up. John McColgan, Larry Masterson and the Deasy brothers, as well as Pat Duffner, were involved – the old brigade! I was disguised as a French soccer supporter, but I knew that if Gay caught a glimpse of my face he would instantly recognise me, despite the disguise and make-up. So we had to choreograph the whole thing.

Gay, who was working with John on a Bord Bainne film, had been told that there was an important piece to be filmed in the main square at Trinity. He was given a script and asked to accessorise it. As he spoke to the camera, I would begin to chant in 'mongrel' French in the background of the shot. As he did more and more 'takes', I got closer and closer to him.

Every time Gay was going to turn around, I turned away with a gesture of defiance or irritation. It worked like a dream, so much so that even I was surprised at Gay's eventual reaction when, after extreme provocation on my part, he asked me, quite irritably, 'Do you understand the English expression "fuck off"?' Afterwards, he was extremely gracious about the whole thing. He thought it was very funny and was more than happy to co-operate.

There were some very memorable candid camera incidents. One of my favourites was the one in the Wax Museum, where I sat – as myself – among effigies of Gay Byrne, Pat Kenny and Pat Ingoldsby and, as people approached, casually said, 'Hello, it's a grand day, isn't it?' The reactions were quite extraordinary!

I also caught out both my father and my mother, on different occasions. We were filming in the Rathgar area one day, and I was dressed in the brown robes of a monk, with wig and spectacles, calling to people's homes and 'auditioning' them for the church choir. When we had finished our scheduled filming, I said to the crew, 'Since we're in the area, let's call around to my mother's house and see if we can catch her out.' So, we set up our blue van outside the house, with the camera carefully concealed as usual. I knocked on the door and Koko, the dog, began to bark. My mother answered the door and, as soon as Koko saw me, he began to jump up at me. My mother kept telling the dog to behave himself, while she greeted me very warmly and asked what she could do for me. I told her I was holding auditions for the church choir and would like to hear her sing, but she said she 'wasn't able to sing at all'. I told her that it was very important that she endeavour to sing, for the glory of God. She was looking closely at me, but I kept my eyes modestly cast down.

'Tell me, Father, what order are you with?' she asked.

'Oh, I'm with the San Franciscans, my child,' I responded, with what I still think of as pretty impressive mental agility. 'Now, my child,' I continued, 'I'd like you to raise the rafters for the Lord.'

'Oh, Father, I couldn't,' she said.

'Come along now, my child,' I insisted. 'The Lord wants to hear the voices of his people raised in prayer.'

'Not at all, Father, I couldn't.'

'Come on, now, my child,' I said in a slightly threatening way. 'Raise the rafters for the Lord. What do you know – the Adeste?'

'Well, I know some of the Adeste,' she said.

'Rightyo, then, my child. Away we go,' and I began to sing. After the first few words, she started to sing, grudgingly and quietly.

'Louder, my child!' I exhorted, 'Louder, for the honour and glory of the Lord.' She obliged. 'Let it all hang out, my child!' I got a little carried away. And she did begin to sing with some bravura. As we approached the end of the first verse, I thought it had gone far enough.

'You haven't got a bad voice at all, Ma, d'you know that?' I said in my own voice.

She stopped, looked at me very intently and said, 'Michael! God, I'll kill you!'

'You'd better take it nice and easy now. You're on television and the van is outside the door taking pictures of you,' I told her.

'I'm on television?' looking at the van. 'God, you're dreadful! Why didn't you tell me you were calling? I wouldn't have worn my apron!' And that was all she was worried about – the fact that she had been caught on television wearing her apron and hadn't had time to get dressed up! She was, however, amused about the whole thing. My father, though, was a different matter.

We were in the vicinity of Harold's Cross and I was dressed to look like a member of the Travelling community. I had a red wig, wellington boots and generally looked a little downbeat. We had already called to a bicycle shop owned by a man I knew, and he hadn't recognised me. Paddy Walsh was his name and he had taken a hammer to me when I suggested that I'd like to test ride one of his bikes around the square before deciding whether I would buy it or not! I then suggested to the crew that, since we were in the vicinity, why wouldn't we call to my father's garage. And so we did. I asked one of his staff if I could talk to 'the boss' and, when he came out to the forecourt, I began to walk around the cars, kicking them and saying, 'That's a bit of an oul' heap of stuff,' but that I 'might buy one all the same'. He was looking at me very carefully. I asked him if I would get a reduction if I paid cash.

'I'd need to see the colour of your money,' he said. I continued to kick the cars.

'I'll tell you what I'll do, boss. I'll take one o' them cars for a drive around the block and then I'll let you know whether I'll buy it or not.'

'Do you know what you'll do,' he said to me, 'You'll fuck off outa here, and you'll do it fast, before I give you a good kick in the arse.'

185

I paused, then said in my own voice, 'Imagine! You'd use that tone of voice to your beloved eldest son!'

He wasn't amused, but he did give us permission to use the item. When the crew had driven away and I was taking my leave of him, he called me over.

'Michael,' he said, 'I want to say one thing to you. In the name of Jaysus, would you get yourself a decent effin' job and stop this messing around on television.' He still didn't see my career in terms of a 'real job'.

There were many good pieces that we filmed but were unable to show because the people involved wouldn't give us written permission. One such occurred exactly a week after I had tricked Gay at Trinity College. I was dressed as a punk rocker and was standing outside the main entrance of Dunnes in Cornelscourt. I was wearing a spiked wig, one half pink, the other green. I had a safety pin in my cheek, paint all over my face, tiny sunglasses, a filthy leather jacket, chains all over me, torn shirt, ripped jeans and Doc Marten boots. All in all, I was quite a sight! The manager of Dunnes was in on the gag, and our van was in the car park, filming. The manager emerged from the main entrance, accompanying a very respectable woman who had a trolley full of goods, and he called me over.

'Stephen, could you ever give this woman a hand to her car with the trolley?'

'Yeah, righ',' I said.

The woman looked at me and said, 'No, thank you very much indeed, I can manage myself.'

'Looka, I have to,' I said, 'It's me job. Where's your car?'

She couldn't let go of the trolley in case I ran off with it, so she held on with one hand as I pushed the trolley aggressively through the car park. The poor woman was mortified. As we passed by a parked car, I gave it a kick.

'It's a disgrace where people park their cars, isn't it?' I said.

With that, Fran Dempsey, wearing a little hat, carrying a briefcase and looking extremely respectable, walked right up to me.

'Excuse me, did you just kick my car?' he said.

'I didn't kick yer car,' I responded aggressively.

'Is he with you?' Fran asked the woman.

'Yeah,' I said, 'I'm her brudder, okay.'

'He is not my brother,' the woman said.

'C'mon, sis,' I said, 'Let's go to the car.'

'I will not go to the car,' she said, 'And give me back my trolley!'

By this time I knew it had gone far enough.

'I'm only joking. I'm Mike Murphy from RTE and the camera is over there,' pointing at the van.

'Well, you chancer! Do you know who I am?'

'No,' I said, 'I don't.'

'I'm Gay Byrne's sister.' And she was! She wanted to maintain her privacy, however, and so she declined to sign the release and the film was never shown. But I received a phone call from Gay that night, wanting to know had I taken out a contract on the entire family and would I be doing the rounds.

Later that day, still in my punk costume and make-up, I got into my car and drove to the Loreto Convent in Foxrock to collect Elaine and Carol for their lunch. I left my car outside, went straight into the vestibule and, in a Dublin accent, asked one of the nuns if Elaine and Carol were ready to come for their dinner. The girls emerged with their friends, all of whom thought that this exotic creature was quite gorgeous. I understand the entire school derived an immense amount of hilarity from the incident, even the nuns.

I have often been asked if I was ever physically accosted during these items, as I sometimes pushed people to the limit. It did happen once, in the Midlands. I had called to a man's house, dressed in my usual scruffy manner, and asked him if he wanted us to tarmacadam his garden. He had a very attractive garden and, quite understandably, he did not fancy a nice smooth dark surface in its place!

'He says it's alright, lads. Yiz can come in now,' I shouted to an imaginary gang.

'I did *not* say it's alright,' he said, 'Get out of my garden!'

'You'se can start immediately, lads. Come on in.'

He became very angry and told me to leave or he would call the police. I totally ignored him.

'That's a desperate looking oul' garden seat you have over there,' I said, walking over to the seat and lifting it onto my shoulder. He ran after me.

'Give that back!' he shouted, taking the garden seat from me and walking back towards his garage with it over his shoulder.

I was unaware at the time that his garden was a prize-winning one and that he had won first prize in a tidy gardens competition, or some such thing, in the Midlands. I had noticed a huge flower in the middle of a flowerbed in the centre of the garden, so, as he was walking towards his garage, I called out 'That's a desperate looking oul' weed you have in the middle. I'll get rid of that for you.' I crossed over to it and bent down as if to rip the flower from the bed, and it was only later, on film, that I saw what happened. He spotted what I was going to do, and fired the garden seat at the garage door. Then he leapt over a rose-bush, ran at me and gave me a 'root' in the behind that nearly put me over the wall. That terminated our filming! I did have the temerity to ask him if he would sign the release form, but he told me that, if I wasn't gone from his garden within ten seconds, he would call the police.

Probably the most tasteless item of all was the one when we borrowed a hearse and coffin. We parked the hearse in Clyde Road and I hopped into the coffin. My two helpers, Dermot Morgan and Fran Dempsey, dressed in suitably sombre fashion, would get the coffin halfway out of the hearse and Dermot would stop a passerby and say, 'Would you mind holding on to the end of this coffin? We just have to go into the house and collect the flowers.' And sometimes a passerby would oblige and hold the end of the coffin, to stop it falling out of the hearse.

As soon as I knew that someone was holding it, I would begin to moan slightly inside the coffin. I could hear the murmurs of 'Oh, Jesus,' from outside. I would start knocking on the lid of the coffin and, if that didn't provoke a reaction, I would start to push up the lid. At that stage, the coffin was usually shoved back into the hearse and the passerby would disappear in a cloud of dust. However, we had to stop the whole thing when one man tried to run off but only got a few yards down the road before collapsing on a wall, gasping for breath. We were the ones who got the fright then! Fortunately, the man was alright and, very sportingly, signed our release form. But that was the end of our work for that day!

I was, however, getting worried that some of the stunts were beginning to border on the sadistic. One day, for instance, we set up in an antiques shop in the centre of the city. I was disguised as the antiques dealer, and we had arranged that a firm of couriers would send over a relay of motorbike messengers to take a valuable vase to another address. When the helmeted youth arrived, I would say, 'There's the vase,' indicating an attractive blue vase on the edge of the table. I would tell him it was worth in the region of a half a million pounds and that I wanted him to deliver it to a certain address.

'Could you please keep an eye on it while I go and get some paper to wrap it in?' I would ask. After I had disappeared into the back room, a trip wire was applied, the table collapsed and the vase broke. By the time I reappeared, the young man, who was being filmed all the time, would be in quite a state. With a number of the couriers we got the results we wanted: some tried to put it back together again, others tried to sweep it under a sideboard so that it wouldn't be noticed and one actually ran out of the shop. But the fourth young man simply stood there and began to cry. He apologised over and over again, said it wasn't his fault and asked us not to report him to his superiors. We immediately called a halt, I apologised to the poor lad and we offered to compensate him for the distress we had caused him.

At lunch that day, I told John Keogh that that was the end of it, I would not be doing any more. And, although some years later I did one or two harmless ones for a specific candid camera series, my appetite was gone and I effectively withdrew from that style of television.

The Follies of Finance (or How I
Learned to Stop Loving Russell Murphy)

After a second highly successful year, *The Live Mike* team broke up, as the crew moved up the corporate ladder. I was, however, asked to do another series and I agreed. I was assigned another producer, John Lynch, and we set to work. The series was, in the main, successful, but there were elements that I did not like. I thought it was sometimes hard-edged and humourless, and lacking in any real creativity. But I know that I shocked everybody as we finished the final programme of the series in that third year. With the then Controller of Programmes, John Kelleher, standing in the studio watching, I announced, live on air, that *The Live Mike* would not be back next year. I thanked those who had taken part and the public for their support. John Kelleher was almost apoplectic. He tackled me immediately afterwards, saying that *he* would decide whether there would be another series, and not me.

The next day, Gay came into my office and asked me if I had gone mad. I told him that I had lost interest in the series, that I felt it had run its course and that I didn't want to do another one. He couldn't believe that I had made such a decision.

'But it's up there at the top of the ratings,' he said. 'There's at least another five years in it. How can you walk away from something as successful as that?'

I told Gay that I had not enjoyed working on this series as much as I had on the earlier ones and that, as far as I was concerned, life was too short to be wasting my time doing things I didn't enjoy. He shook his head, baffled, but offered me all his support, even though he reiterated that he simply couldn't understand how I could abandon such a successful show.

This whole episode served to make me reflect on my career. I had become a broadcaster more or less by accident, but had found that I enjoyed the work and the variety immensely. I also realised that I needed change as part of my professional life, that I got bored after a while and that, once I lost interest, the quality of my work began to suffer. But I also made a very important discovery. I realised that, through broadcasting, I was able to do many of the things I wanted to do. In other words, I had the means at my disposal to explore myself, my attitudes, my abilities, and the world. I was able to learn, and to exercise my mother's dictum about seeing 'as much of God's earth as you possibly can'. The fact that I could successfully transmit my enjoyment to a significant number of listeners and viewers was a bonus. I suspect that they derived some pleasure from accompanying me on what was, and is, a fairly exhilarating ride.

I have never considered myself to be egotistical and I certainly don't think of myself in terms of being a *great* broadcaster, but I derive immense pleasure from my work. I do not seek publicity, I avoid crowds and find being described as a 'television personality' somewhat embarrassing (I prefer the term broadcaster). I realise how fortunate I am that my work coincides with my interests, pastimes and chosen lifestyle.

It was during the early eighties that my relationship with Russell Murphy came to an end. I had met Russell during the time I was working with Brendan Smith. He was one of Brendan's great friends and was a major supporter of the Dublin Theatre Festival. When I was eighteen or nineteen, Russell suggested that if I needed any accountancy advice he would be happy to oblige, and so, almost by default, he became my accountant! I found him to be a delightfully amusing character. His appearance alone was quite striking. Tall – about six-foot-three – somewhat stooped, with a shock of carefully combed black hair, a long, lugubrious, sharp-featured face with intelligent eyes, and a deep sonorous voice. He always dressed in black: a long black coat, usually with a velvet collar, often simply thrown over his shoulders, black suit, black tie, white shirt. He was a cross between the archetypal banker and the 'grand actor' of the old school. And I think that is how he saw himself. I believe Russell *played* the role of an accountant, but that his real passion was for theatre, radio and television.

He had garnered for himself a pretty distinguished bunch of clients, in name anyway, but I doubt if the income he officially received from them was very substantial. It was proven much later, of course, that his 'unconventional earnings' from these clients was pretty impressive. Among them were names like T P McKenna, Hugh Leonard, Gay Byrne, Brian Farrell and, latterly, Frank Hall.

Russell liked to impress with his generosity. There would be two tickets in the post for the Gate Theatre during the Theatre Festival. There would be a birthday card with a box of chocolates for Eileen, and Gay would tell me about Russell's extraordinary generosity to Kathleen and their daughters. I remember Gay telling me once that Russell had phoned him to say that he thought Kathleen was looking a little 'peaky' and that he had arranged for her to fly to London with the two girls. A limousine picked them up at the airport and took them to an expensive hotel, where they spent the weekend. Gay was deeply touched by Russell's generosity at the time and it was only many years later that I thought about the consternation it must have caused Gay to discover that it was his own money that had paid for these luxuries!

I had often visited Russell in his office and always quite enjoyed the theatricality of the meeting. He would wear a long, fairly threadbare beige or grey cardigan over his white shirt, black tie and black trousers, and would constantly pace the room. He would hold his palm to his brow as he worked out a complicated tax problem for me. He would wander towards the window, stand behind me and occasionally kneel at the desk in deep contemplation. I was quite accustomed to his demeanour, as indeed I was to the religious emblems that he kept in full view in his office, little statues, rosary beads and so on, and I always looked forward to these meetings with him. He seemed to think everything was possible, that money was a mere irritant that got in the way of fulfilling one's dreams and he tried to make me believe that I simply had to decide what I wanted and the means to get it would naturally follow.

Once every year, Russell would gather together his 'artistic' clients and we would go out for a meal. Initially the venue was the old Jury's Hotel in Dame Street, then the Moira Hotel, then the Lord Edward and, when it opened, Bloom's Hotel. On all of these occasions it would be my mission to try to get Gay to buy a round of drinks. It became a standing joke between Gay and me. He knew I would try to set him up and he would protest and try to get out of buying the round. Eventually, one year in Bloom's Hotel, I made an announcement to everyone present.

'This is the year that Gay is buying a round,' and Gay capitulated.

'All right then,' he said, 'What are you all having?'

I said that I would have a large brandy and white lemonade, and I exhorted the others not to stint themselves. Nor did they! The drinks were all served and Gay, still protesting, opened his wallet and addressed the barman.

'How much do I owe you?' he asked.

'Not at all,' said the barman grandly, 'Since it's yourself, Mr Byrne, the drinks are on the house.' Gay thanked him profusely and promptly put the ten-pound note back in his wallet.

'There you are,' he said. 'And a very happy Christmas to you all!'

Russell had suggested to Gay that it would probably be in his best interests if he, Russell, were to negotiate Gay's contract with RTE. By that stage, it seemed logical that Russell would also negotiate mine. Another popular broadcaster at the time was Frank Hall, and Gay and I thought it would be a good idea if Frank were also brought into the 'fold'. When I asked Frank if he would be interested in Russell negotiating for him, Frank readily agreed, and so Russell took the bit between his teeth and sashayed in for the 'kill'.

Vincent Finn was the Director-General of RTE at the time, Muiris MacConghail was Controller of Programmes in television and Michael Carroll was Controller of Programmes in radio. It was Vincent's wish that Gerry McLaughlin, an acerbic, tough Scottish lawyer who was the Head of Contracts, would be part of the negotiations. Russell, however, without meeting Gerry, informed RTE that he did not want the lawyer at any of their meetings, and RTE chose to fudge the question for the time being.

There followed an extraordinary sequence of events. Russell, who was always chauffeur-driven to meetings, arrived at RTE to negotiate with Vincent Finn. His car drew up at the entrance to the administration building, but he remained in the car. After five minutes, Russell ordered his driver to take him back to the city. He telephoned Gay, myself and Frank, and informed us that, since the Director-General of RTE had not seen fit to greet him – the representative of the 'three foremost broadcasters' in the station – in person, at the door of the administration building, that Russell had decided he would not demean himself by simply arriving at reception and asking to be shown upstairs!

We were all taken aback at this high-handed action, and even more so when we heard that Russell had dispatched a stinging letter by hand to Vincent Finn, informing him that in future he expected to be met personally by the Director-General at the entrance to RTE and escorted to wherever the negotiations were to take place.

Vincent Finn was one of the most popular Director-Generals RTE ever had. A retiring, pleasant and very approachable man, he ran the organisation quietly and efficiently. He was always courteous and I had never heard of him raising his voice in anger. However, the reports we received within RTE were that Vincent was quite incensed about the incident. He did, however, contact Russell's office a few weeks later to say that he would be happy to meet with him at a time and a place convenient to Russell. The meeting was arranged for ten o'clock on a Saturday morning at Russell's office (at Russell's behest) and Vincent was effectively told, by Russell, to *be* there, to be *on time*, and *not* to bring the lawyer. Why he had this attitude to Gerry, I don't know. He had not met him, but McLaughlin is known as a formidable, no-nonsense, utterly candid man.

I had recently been approached by BBC Pebble Mill to present their major New Year's Eve television programme. I had already been over once or twice to record interviews for the programme with people like Andy Williams and Diana Dors and generally I was getting on very well with the BBC. I was in Birmingham on this particular night before Christmas, having just finished a recording, when I received a phone call from Fred O'Donovan, the Chairman of RTE. By then the contract negotiations had been dragging on over a long period of time, and Gay, myself and Frank had decided to take a fairly hard line. Gay, who was scheduled to do *The Late Late Show* on the Saturday, had intimated to RTE that, unless a satisfactory resolution was reached, he would not appear. Fred, with whom I had been friends for a long time, told me what had happened in Russell's office that Saturday morning.

Vincent Finn had turned up at the appointed time at Russell's office, but had also brought Gerry McLaughlin. The two of them were kept waiting in an outer office for over half an hour. They were offered neither coffee nor newspapers. Eventually, Russell's secretary came out and asked them their names. Twenty minutes later, Russell himself appeared and informed them that, as Mr McLaughlin was present, the meeting would not now take place and that they were free to go. Fred told me that the RTE delegation felt insulted and humiliated, and that they were reaching the stage where they were going to let all three of us go! He asked me to ring Gay to have a chat with him, which I did.

'Listen,' I said, 'This kind of nonsense is no way to conduct negotiations. I think Russell is for the birds, the way he's behaving.'

Gay didn't completely agree, but he did think that Russell had gone too far. The three of us told Russell to moderate his actions, and, although he was extremely disgruntled about what he saw as a softening in our approach to RTE, he half-heartedly finalised our contracts – and Gay appeared on *The Late Late Show* the following Saturday.

My relationship with Russell ended about two years before his death. Eileen and I had moved from Kerrymount in Foxrock to a house in Carrickmines and had bought the house in our usual way – haphazardly! I went to view it, told Eileen it was lovely and then headed off on, I think, a Eurovision trip. I told Eileen to go along to the auction, see what the house was going for and make a decision accordingly. So, she went along and suddenly found herself the proud owner of a run-down old house in the suburb of Carrickmines. My reactions were mixed when she phoned to tell me the good news; firstly because of the cost of the place (it was around seventy thousand pounds, which was a lot of money then) and secondly because of the amount of work the house needed.

Russell had handled the whole thing and, after about six months, I found that there was a substantial amount of money unaccounted for. This reactivated suspicions I had had over the last few years of my dealings with Russell and I decided to confront him, although frankly the prospect did not appeal to me. Eileen had never met him, despite the boxes of chocolates he had sent her, but she offered to come with me to see if she could help sort things out.

We went up to his office, where I was greeted like a lord. Eileen, having been welcomed enthusiastically, was seated on a hard-backed chair in the corner of Russell's office, while he ushered me to his own seat behind the desk, to allow him space in which to pace and posture.

'What's the problem, dear boy?' he asked. I mumbled something about some money being missing and wanting to check it out.

'Money missing?' he mused. 'Well, tell me about it.'

He wandered over to the window and opened it, a small window overlooking a fairly grubby side street landscape in the city centre, and sat with his bottom sticking out of the window and his chin in his hand, looking at me. I explained that there was a good deal of money over the years that I needed to talk to him about, and he mused, 'Hmm . . . really?' for a while.

He stood up, walked thoughtfully across the little office and back, murmuring, 'We'll have to look into this. We'll have to be more specific.' He took his rosary beads from his pocket, as he was wont to do, and which was no surprise to me, wound them around his fingers and continued to pace slowly. Eileen was mesmerised by this performance. He then knelt opposite me, with his elbows on the desk, staring all the while into my eyes, and asked me a number of questions while winding the rosary beads thoughtfully around his fingers. I answered, defensively, as best I could and it was agreed that he would look into what was 'a very serious matter indeed'. We shook hands elaborately, thanked each other very much, hoped we weren't wasting each other's time, and Eileen and I left.

As we were walking down the stairs, I said to Eileen, who was rather quiet, 'He's a bit unusual, isn't he?'

'A bit unusual?' she said. 'He's a complete head case! We should get rid of him fast.' And we did. We cut our losses, quite unsatisfactorily, and, to Russell's deep resentment, I terminated my business relationship with him and went to a new accountant. Years later, when I heard that Russell was dying, I asked Gay to give him my best regards. However, when I next saw Gay he told me that Russell had said he didn't want 'that Judas' to visit him while he was ill.

The BBC had now begun to take a serious interest in my career. Bob Langley, who was the presenter of the *Saturday Night at the Mill* show, had decided to leave and a replacement was being sought. It was intimated that they were interested in me, and that, if I handled the New Year's Eve show well, the job was mine. As it turned out, the show went very satisfactorily and the critics were extremely kind as well. Within a couple of weeks, Pebble Mill offered me the job. I told them I might have problems regarding my contract with RTE as I would be presenting the BBC's late-night Saturday show, which would be in direct conflict with Gay on RTE. I spoke with Muiris MacConghail and he said the problem might not be insurmountable and he would think about it.

A few days later, I received a phone call from a senior executive at BBC Pebble Mill who told me that headquarters in London had instructed them that under no circumstances was I to be contracted by Pebble Mill. I was taken aback at the abruptness and finality of the message and was subsequently informed that there were 'pressures brought to bear' on the BBC to keep me off the air. Was this true? I don't know. Where did this pressure come from? I don't know that either.

I did not consider it to be a huge career setback, however, because I was not greatly enamoured with the prospect of working in England. I was quite happy with my life and career at the time and the move would only have meant major hassles with RTE, having to get to grips with a whole new broadcasting environment and possibly even moving the family. Nonetheless, I had satisfied myself that I was well able to survive in the cross-channel arena.

Loss and Oz

On 27 December 1981, while I was recording for the Pebble Mill New Year's Eve programme, my father died. After my mother's death he had stayed on for a while in Vernon Grove, where John still lived, and Auntie May used to come in to cook the meals. It soon became obvious that the house was too big for the two of them and so my father decided to sell.

On the day of Ma's funeral, he had created considerable resentment among his children because he insisted that his friend Mary, a very nice woman whom we had all met, would accompany him to my house where we all adjourned in the evening. We all considered this action to be insensitive and inappropriate, and it caused a lot of tension.

Two years before his death I had received a phone call late one night to come to Baggot Street Hospital as Da had been involved in a car crash. I was the first of the family to arrive and I got a shock when I saw him. He had been driving down a side road in Churchtown in a Mini – he never owned his own car, he would simply take whatever was available in the garage – when another driver reversed from his driveway into his path. Da hadn't seen the other car, and he ploughed straight into it and was thrown partly through the windscreen. His face and head were in a terrible mess, he had glass in his eye and I could see little else but blood. He was conscious, but in shock. When, with his one good eye, he saw me come into the room, he did a most unusual thing. He grasped me by the shoulder, mumbling, 'Michael, am I going to be alright?' I tried to reassure him as best I could before they took him away for surgery.

His face and head had to be stitched and he had numerous operations on his eye. However, in time it got better and his face healed, but the accident had had a debilitating effect on his health. Over the next couple of years, he had a heart attack, then another, and was in and out of hospital. Apart from this he lived his life as he had always done. He had sold the garage but was still employed by the new owners, T R Motors, as a salesman and he continued to work late at night and finish up with a few drinks. He moved into 'digs' with friends of his, invariably women. I'm not sure if he had any intimate relationships, although he had many female friends. Certainly, there were many women who sought his company.

He kept in touch with his children on a regular basis – with me through Eileen, who was very fond of him and with whom he had an excellent relationship. He often visited our house, where he and I gave each other space so that he could function as the good grandfather he turned out to be. He was, I gather from other sources, extremely happy about my career. He often told people how proud he was, how he hadn't thought I would amount to much and how pleased he was at my success. But he never mentioned it to me.

He had buried his own mother who lived to the age of ninety-nine, early in 1981, the same year in which he himself was to die. Inadvertently, there was considerable family merriment at Gran's funeral. There was no room for me in the back of the chief mourners' car and so I had to sit at the front with the driver, who was a suitably dour, lugubrious fellow who hadn't much conversation. As we were driving, behind the hearse, out to Deansgrange cemetery, I observed, for want of something to say, that his must be an interesting profession. He had a 'posh' Dublin accent and had obviously worked on upgrading it.

'Oh yes,' he said, 'Very interesting indeed. We do come across some unusual cases, I must say.' Now I couldn't stop him. 'I am reminded,' he went on, 'of an occasion not long ago when we were called to a house where the late lamented had passed away upstairs. It was a small house and the late lamented was an elderly gentleman with two grown-up sons, one of whom was upstairs and the other downstairs. We put the late lamented into a box – not as grand a box as your grandmother has, but a fairly flimsy job – and commenced carrying the box down the stairs. I was below and my colleague was above and, as we descended, I inadvertently slipped, causing my colleague to lose his footing. I stumbled further and the box, containing the late lamented, flew over my head and down the stairs. There was a terrible commotion. The son who was upstairs shouted, "Jaysus, me father's after fallin' down the stairs!" and the son who was downstairs came running out and said, "Oh Christ, is he all right?"'

He hadn't so much as cracked a smile while he told the story, but the car was rocking with the laughter of the entire family. Flushed with success, my new-found friend went on to enquire if I had ever encountered a 'dressed grave'. I told him I hadn't.

'A dressed grave is used,' he went on to explain, 'when somebody of great import dies. Palm fronds are put across the top of the grave so that the relatives don't see the muck being thrown on top of the box. Usually, because it's somebody very important, there's a big crowd around. We attended a funeral at Glasnevin Cemetery recently with a Very Important Personage behind in the box. The dressed grave, where the VIP was to be buried, was on the right-hand side and there was a huge crowd of people with a number of gardaí around the grave. When we brought out the late lamented, we were interrupted by a shout. Everything stopped, but nobody knew what was happening. Then somebody noticed a hat clutched in a hand, waving above the palm fronds. Hadn't one of the guards fallen into the grave and was trying to attract attention.'

We were approaching Deansgrange by now, and even my father was laughing out loud.

Despite Gran's contrariness, he had been very good to her. She was in an old folk's home in Donnybrook when Declan came back to Ireland as a priest. Nothing would do but that her grandson should come into the home and celebrate mass. Declan was delighted to oblige. While he said the mass, our grandmother sat about a third of the way down the small chapel. As was customary with the Legionaries of Christ, Declan gave a good deal of time to the celebration. He left long pauses and was quietly reverent and dignified. When he came to the elevation, he slowly intoned the first part and then left a pause for meditation. After a moment or two, my grandmother's voice rang out in the church.

'This is the cup of my blood,' she called irritably. 'I say, this is the cup of my blood.' She thought Declan had forgotten the next part and was prompting him. Declan caught my eye and grinned.

'Thank you, Gran,' he said, and continued with the mass.

Da was found dead in bed. It was John who found him. Pat had phoned him to say that she had received a call telling her that he hadn't turned up for a lunch appointment. John apparently said to his wife, Lisanne, 'Da's dead.' He went over to the house, but there was no response to his knock. He made a few phone calls, the owner arrived and together they went into Da's room. He was lying on his side, looking extremely peaceful, having died in his sleep.

It was a peaceful end to what appeared to me to have been a fairly unsatisfactory life. But then I knew so little about him. He loved the motor business; he was extremely popular with people; he enjoyed a few drinks; he could tell a great story; he was very good with children – other people's children that is. The only major blemish on his life seems to have been his marriage, and the consequent unpleasant atmosphere in the home. He must have regretted marrying my mother. He must have been disturbed about the lack of communication between himself and his children. He must have had deeply unhappy moments. But, if he did, he never spoke to any of us about it. He never spoke ill of my mother after she died, beyond saying that she could be a difficult woman at times.

I deeply regret that I never got to know him, that he never insisted I should get to know him. I feel sure I would have liked him, maybe even loved him. He has profoundly affected me all my life. His shadow dominated my childhood and has kept pace with me through adulthood. The discovery, years later, that he was not the malign presence my mother had painted, has left me with a painfully unresolved dimension to my life. I am emotionally affected, even at movies, if I see a young boy being treated with unkindness or cruelty, or if I see his feelings being abused. I am deeply affected as I write these words. It's the *sadness* of it, the fact that he *allowed* his eldest son, and all of his children in one way or another, to be turned against him; that he did so without protest, without fighting for our love or our approval. He simply gave up and retreated into a sullen, dark and threatening presence. I still meet people who tell me what a wonderful man my father was and I always say yes, I know. But I don't. I didn't know him.

When my marriage was in the process of breaking up, I did something I thought I would never allow myself to do. I went into psychotherapy. I did not want help from a misty-eyed do-gooder who would put a box of Kleenex in front of me and invite me to open my heart. I wanted someone who would challenge me and who would be capable of holding their own if the situation turned nasty. I knew there was a lot of pent-up resentment and confusion behind my professional façade and that it would be painful if the mask was removed. I found an unusual Dutchman named Fierman Bennink Bolt who lives in Dún Laoghaire. Fierman is abrasive, direct, even cranky at times, hates small talk and, most importantly, he hadn't a clue who Mike Murphy was.

It took him a long time to break down my inhibitions, but, when he finally did, I learned how to cope in a better way with the perceived injustices and the regrets of my early life. And he helped me to come to terms with my once all-consuming resentment of my father.

My children were beginning to find their feet by the time my father died. They had grown up with the fact that their father was famous, and that their time with him in public was always going to be prone to interruption. I still ache when I remember one manifestation of this. I had taken my daughter Deirdre to the zoo and the two of us were standing outside the monkeys' cages when a throng of schoolchildren surrounded me. Deirdre was three, maybe four, at the time and was holding my hand. The kids were all very excited; they had seen me on television and they wanted my autograph. They were screaming, chattering and proffering pieces of paper and I was doing my best to oblige them, and to take care of Dee at the same time. I felt her little hand slipping from mine and I told her to hold on to my trousers while I signed the autographs. I continued signing for a few minutes, then looked up and saw Dee standing about thirty yards away, outside the group, looking at me with an expression of bewilderment and dismay. I ran to her and picked her up.

It was a seminal moment for both of us. I recognised how fragile my relationship with my children was, and how important it was in comparison with the frivolous side of being a so-called 'TV personality'. The look on Deirdre's face had frightened me; it was a look of grief, almost of loss. She still remembers the incident very clearly and has confirmed what I felt. For Dee it brought about the realisation that her father wasn't like other fathers, that he belonged, or seemed to belong, to a lot more people than just the immediate family. Dee recalls that that incident determined her subsequent reluctance, throughout her childhood and teenage years, to accompany me anywhere in public on her own.

My two eldest daughters, Elaine and Carol, had a happy, well-adjusted childhood. Eileen and I spoiled them, if anything, and I created an environment that was good-humoured, if, as I have mentioned before, somewhat superficial. From the time they were nine or ten years of age, I used to take them with me every Saturday morning around the commercial art galleries in Dublin. They became quite proficient in identifying a Paul Henry or a Patrick Collins. We did this every week, for six or seven years, until inevitably, in their teens, they told me in no uncertain terms that they had other and better things to do with their Saturday mornings. They had discovered an extraordinary phenomenon called 'boys' and these were much more interesting than Irish artists!

Mark was always good with his hands. He enjoyed taking things, like little electrical cars, to pieces and putting them back together again. For a period he was an avid Liverpool supporter, but lost interest when he discovered music. He is now a highly accomplished guitarist and is working in Temple Bar in the music industry. I am extremely proud of him, as I am of my daughters. Elaine, Carol and Deirdre, who love travel and new experiences, have all lived in the United States at various times, and thoroughly enjoyed being there. They have all now returned home and settled, for the present anyway, in Ireland.

In 1984, I decided to change my professional life. I was becoming bored with broadcasting and doing the same thing over and over again. I realised that simply being a television and radio performer was not enough for me and that I needed to develop another dimension to my life. I proceeded to look around for something new.

Pat Murphy, who had succeeded Michael Scott, the architect, as Chairman of ROSC, the international art exhibition, invited me to join the committee for the forthcoming ROSC. I was delighted, because my interest in the visual arts was now very important to me. I went to

Edinburgh to present a week of radio programmes from the festival that year and, while there, met the remarkable arts entrepreneur, Richard Demarco, and his assistant, Jane MacAllister. They were doing amazing things on a very small budget in their studio complex. Richard had a reputation for experimentation, for adventurous entrepreneurship, and he had fostered the burgeoning Eastern European arts community. It was he who introduced Joseph Beuys, the conceptual artist, and Tadeusz Kantor, the great theatre director to the West.

I returned to Dublin fired with enthusiasm, determined to initiate something new that would reflect my faith in Dublin as a European cultural centre. The result was an all-encompassing festival which I named ContemporÉire – a clever little artistic pun, I thought at the time, though now it seems vaguely pretentious. I gathered together people like Michael Colgan from the Gate Theatre, an old friend whom I greatly admire, and Lewis Clohessy, a first-class arts administrator, artist Gerald Davis and academic Rosemarie Mulcahy, the young architect Shane O'Toole and many other like-minded souls. We approached Bord Fáilte, Dublin Tourism and many other bodies and found that they were receptive to the idea. We also brought in James Delaney, who was best known as the Texan who bought the Battle of the Boyne site. He agreed to finance 'Green on the Screen', which became the first ever Dublin Film Festival.

Unfortunately, that year the Dublin Theatre Festival, through lack of finance and, I think, a little mismanagement, was cancelled, and suddenly ContemporÉire was bereft of one of its two central pillars (the other being ROSC). However, we did manage to put together a very exciting programme of events: the first ever Dublin street carnival; an immensely successful conference on Art and the Human Environment, with people like Gough Whitlam, the ex-Prime Minister of Australia; Anthony Burgess delivered one of the best papers I have ever heard on Joyce and Dublin; artists Joseph Beuys, Richard Serra, Dani Karavan were there, as was Jack Lang, the radical French Minister for Culture. Charlie Haughey spoke and so did Garret FitzGerald, Ruairi Quinn, and many others. There were concerts, plays, street shows, banquets, and a whole host of items that enlivened the city for a few weeks in October.

The head of Dublin Tourism, Matt McNulty, who is now the chief executive of Bord Fáilte, gave us tremendous encouragement and practical assistance. He lent us offices in Dublin Tourism's building and, by the time Lewis had wrapped up fiscal matters, we actually finished up a hundred pounds in the black. Through ContemporÉire, a number of artistic careers were launched. Jane Daly, now running Druid in Galway, started there, as did Grace Perrott, Myra Geraghty, and many others.

It was a challenging venture and unbelievably time-consuming, but in the end it was well worth it. I had based the premise of ContemporÉire on my belief, as I was quoted as saying at the time, that Dublin was on the brink of a cultural renaissance. I truly believed we were on the edge of something great, and this belief has been vindicated over recent years. I like to think that I was one of the first to recognise that Dublin could compete culturally and architecturally with the world's best.

The world of the arts is not always sweet and cerebral. There is a hard, ruthless and often crooked side as well. There are unscrupulous dealers who knowingly buy and sell fakes, and who, in some cases, will pay artists to counterfeit paintings. Some years ago, I did business with a certain art dealer. I had bought a number of paintings from him and had put him in touch with friends who also bought from him. I discovered that some of the paintings he had sold me were fakes and challenged him about it, but he was not willing to compensate me. I told him that I wanted satisfaction, but he did nothing for over a year.

It was then brought to my attention that a painting that I had had for a long time, and which I had also bought from him, was yet another skilful forgery. I told him that this time I was going to take action. Again, he pleaded ignorance and did nothing. A month or so later, he phoned me, with astonishing effrontery, to tell me that he had been asked to sell a painting by Walter Osborne, worth about fifty thousand pounds, and enquired if I knew of a client for it? He had four days in which to sell the painting and he would then have to return it to its owner. I thought about it for a couple of hours and then decided to play fire with fire. I called him and said that I might have a potential buyer but that I would need to keep the painting overnight. He agreed. I called to his office, collected the painting and took it straight to a bank, where I lodged it for safety. I then phoned him and he agreed to see me the next morning, thinking I had found a buyer.

The next day, I met him in his office and told him that there was a problem.

'No, there's no problem,' he said, 'If your friend doesn't like it, it doesn't matter.'

At this point I informed him that he was the one with the problem, that the painting was somewhere safe and that, unless he paid me a certain sum of money in cash, he would not see the painting again. I reminded him that there was no paperwork to prove that I had the Osborne and that there would be no further mention of the picture from me – that I wouldn't know what he was talking about. He was naturally extremely angry. I told him he had thirty-six hours in which to pay me the money and I would then arrange for the painting's return, but that I would be making no further contact with him.

I did not hear from him for two days, during which time I was getting a little edgy myself, reflecting on the possible consequences of my actions. Eventually, however, he phoned and said he would meet me at the bank the next morning, which he did. I checked that he had the money and we both went into the vaults and exchanged the picture for the money. Disgraceful behaviour all round, you might say. And you would be right!

After the success of ContemporÉire, I decided to branch out. I spoke with Seamus Deasy, who was one of the top cameramen in Ireland, about forming a production company, and we agreed to go into partnership. When we went to open an account at the bank, we had not yet thought of a company name and so, on the spur of the moment, we came up with the fairly uninspired title 'Emdee Productions' (M for Murphy, D for Deasy – get it?!) That was the uneventful beginning of what is now one of the country's most successful independent production companies.

Larry Masterson, who had become a good friend, was feeling slightly disenchanted with his prospects within RTE, and we discussed the possibility of doing something together. An opportunity presented itself when Aer Lingus announced they were going to introduce films on their flights. By now Lewis Clohessy had joined us as a fellow director. We took a gamble and, in two weeks, made a 20-minute travelogue-style film about Ireland, with commercials. We borrowed £25,000 to make it, and then tried to persuade Aer Lingus to buy it. At first they said no, and I remember Larry and I spending a gruelling weekend, realising that, if this didn't literally *fly*, we could be in serious financial difficulties. However, Aer Lingus eventually agreed to take the film and so Emdee Productions was formally launched. I recall Larry and myself sitting with our feet up on our respective desks, in our brand new office in Haddington Road, without even a sheet of paper between us. Larry picked up a paper clip from the table and held it up.

'This is the beginning of the new company. Let's hope it amounts to something more!'

We made a number of successful corporate films and moved office to Fitzwilliam Square. The building was owned by a friend of mine, Noel Smyth, who was then an aspiring young solicitor. He subsequently had the distinction of being legal advisor to both Don Tidey and Ben Dunne, this despite the fact that Quinnsworth and Dunnes Stores were, commercially at least, in opposition. He currently effectively owns Dunloe House, the publicly quoted property vehicle, as well as being involved in countless other business and commercial entities. Within a year, Emdee, with our partner Noel Smyth, approached RTE to become involved in a six-part series called *Murphy's Australia*.

I had effectively taken a sabbatical from television by now. I presented *Murphy's Microquiz* for a number of years and did sundry other programmes, but nothing very major. One programme I did present and enjoyed for a few years was *Screen Test*, a talent contest in which a panel of 'experts' made comments, sometimes extremely acerbic comments, about the various acts. This series ran for three years and, on the final night of the third series, I performed my old termination routine once again. Vincent Finn, who was then Director-General of RTE, had just presented the award to the overall winner.

As I closed the programme, I said, 'And that brings us to the end of *Screen Test*. We won't be back again next year.'

Once again, there was some dismay among the executive staff, who had made no such decision, but I knew that the series had run its course and that any more would have been nothing less than embarrassing.

My radio career now consisted of afternoon and lunchtime programmes, all easy enough to do and, frankly, somewhat boring for me (I won't question how boring it was for the listeners!)

However, I was very keen to do *Murphy's Australia*. RTE knew, based on the success of *Murphy's America*, that I could do this kind of programme and do it well, but they were extremely reluctant to release me for three months or more, which is what it would take to film such a series, from my radio and television commitments. This was, and still is, extremely frustrating for me. At first, the *Murphy's Australia* project was rejected out of hand, but then I had a number of brainstorming sessions with Noel Smyth, who eventually came up with an attractive proposal, whereby RTE would receive a major series in six parts, effectively for the price of one. Noel had structured it as a tax write-off for one of his clients, who was very pleased to find a vehicle to effect a tax reduction. It was such a complicated deal that the RTE people involved in the financial negotiations later admitted to me that even they didn't fully understand it!

And so it was that we went to Australia. As with America, the whole trip was like manna from heaven for me. Larry was there as producer, my old friend John McColgan was director, Seamus Deasy was on camera, Brendan, his brother, was on sound and Maurice Swan, a former soccer player, was on lighting. Our production assistants over the two trips were Laura McAuley and Judy Murray. My pal Bill O'Herlihy, who had brought in British Airways as sponsors, was also with us for a few weeks. It was a wonderful team, all experienced professionals and very enthusiastic. The weather was fabulous and we received tremendous co-operation wherever we went.

We all fell in love with Perth, the most remote city in the world. Perth is, in fact, closer to Singapore than it is to any other Australian city. In Perth we met an Irishman, Dennis Horgan, who owned a winery, as it is called, on the Margaret River, four hundred miles south of Perth. Dennis, a multimillionaire – like so many other people at that time in Perth – liked to do something spectacular every year for the Perth Arts Festival, and that year he had chartered a jumbo jet to bring the Swedish Symphony Orchestra to play in his winery. In a natural open-air amphitheatre, the orchestra, in full evening dress, proceeded to play Mendelssohn, Mozart and Haydn. The sun was beating down and the kookaburras, those noisy native birds, accompanied the music, to everyone's amusement. As the guests arrived, they were each given a wine glass on a leather strap which they could wear around their necks. While the music played, waiters wandered among the audience, who were sitting or lying on the grass in skimpy summer clothes (some skimpier than others) plying them with more wine. It was a wonderfully bizarre and exhilarating experience.

We went pearl fishing off the 'top end', or northern coast, and we traced Crocodile Dundee's steps through the rainforests. We also met a man who had been part of a group that had been attacked by a crocodile, a story I recalled having read in the newspapers back home. This man, John, was a hunter and guide, and had been having a few drinks with some friends on the banks of the River Daintree, up in the rainforests in the north. It was Christmas Day, the weather was sweltering and he and another male friend unwisely decided to walk into the river, up to their thighs, to cool down as they drank their beers. A woman friend of theirs wanted to join them in the river, but they advised her not to as there might be crocodiles in the vicinity. She told them that two big, strong men like them would be able to protect her and she stepped into the water. They all stood there drinking for a while, the two men facing her, with their backs to the river. Suddenly, a huge crocodile crashed between the two men, knocking them aside like skittles, and lunged at the woman. It took hold of her around the hips and carried her, screaming, into the river. The woman was never seen again. Some bones were subsequently found a long way down the river which could have been hers, and they did eventually shoot what they thought was the 'killer croc', but John had never recovered. He was still quite moved as he spoke about the incident and he refused to tell us the story 'on camera'.

We experienced the exhilaration of a cattle and buffalo round-up on the open plains. This was done in jeeps and helicopters, as well as on horseback. Some of the helicopters were flown by boys as young as sixteen to eighteen years of age – one of them, I recall, in his bare feet! Those kids could manoeuvre the choppers like nothing you've ever seen and I held my breath as my sixteen-year-old pilot plummeted vertically into a clump of trees to scare out the cattle and water-buffalo. The jeeps, meantime, were speeding through the long grass, which was sometimes up to ten feet high. The landscape was dotted with ant-hills, many of them twenty or thirty feet high and almost cement-like in structure. These kids drove the jeeps kamikaze-style, hoping to avoid the ant-hills, and not always succeeding! By the end of the day, there were two broken legs, a set of damaged ribs and numerous gashes and abrasions.

As well as riding in a chopper and a jeep, I rode a horse during the round-up. Naturally, it ran away with me, but at least this time I was able to stay on until it was exhausted and faltered to a stop.

We interviewed some transsexuals at a seedy nightclub in King's Cross in Sydney, we went surfing, also near Sydney, and, finally, we went scuba diving off the Barrier Reef. I recall that dive very well. It wasn't the clearest of days underwater, but, by Irish standards, visibility was excellent! My sub-aqua guide, Danny, gestured to me when we were about eighty feet down that I should feed a moray eel with some fish food that we had brought with us. The eel, with a head the size of a rugby ball, emerged from a gap in the rocks and snapped the food from my hand. Then I saw a long silver fish directly above me and held out some more food. It streaked in, grabbed the food and was gone. I also spotted some sharks in the distance. By the time I reached the surface, I had used almost all of my air through hyperventilating with excitement.

'That was a close call you had with the barracuda,' Danny said.

'What barracuda?' I asked in astonishment.

'That was a barracuda,' he said, 'The one that took the fish from your hand. You were lucky you didn't lose your hand as well!'

When we got home, Pat Duffner, whose magic editing touch was to bring him to Hollywood with *My Left Foot* and many other feature movies, applied his intelligent craftsmanship; and the result was another Jacob's Award.

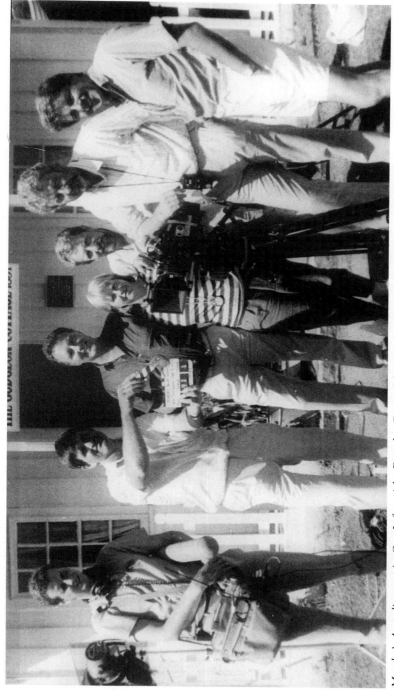

Murphy's Australia team in Oz. *Left to right:* Brendan Deasy, Maurice Swan, myself, Laura McAuley, Larry Masterson, Seamus Deasy and John McColgan.

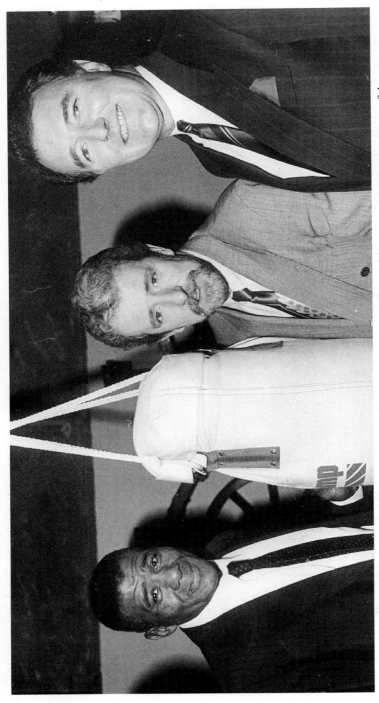

One of the early Emdee successes was *Champions*. We flew our crew around the world to meet great sportspersons of the past. Former Heavyweight Champion, Floyd Patterson (*left*) joined us in Dublin for the launch. Larry Masterson is seen here about to launch a surprise right cross to Patterson's head from behind the punchbag.

The Jacobs Radio and Television Awards 1980. Particularly pleasurable because John McColgan also won an award, as did my good friend John Skehan.

En famille (almost) to the Abbey. *Left to right:* Elaine, Deirdre, Eileen, myself and Mark. Carol is absent.

Family portrait. *Left to right:* (back) Carol, myself, Deirdre; (front) Elaine, Eileen and Mark. This picture induces cringe reactions from the younger fry!

The Murphy Kids all grown up. *Left to right:* Declan, Catherine, myself, Patricia and John.

Brenda Fricker had the Oscar a full five seconds before Eileen 'borrowed' it for the 'snap'.

'Me an' Him' in the Abbey (for a radio programme, I must admit — The G.B. Show's production of *Playboy of the Western World*). About our performances: 'glittering', 'incredibly talented', 'remarkable interpretations', 'acting *tour de force*' were some of the phrases not used by the critics.

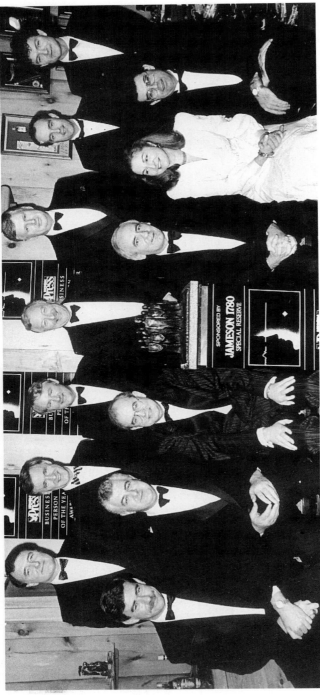

Jameson/Irish Press Business Person of the Year Awards 1990. I was genuinely proud to be selected as a finalist among so many distinguished 'Captains of Industry'!

Included with me are: Maria and Pat Cooney (Tipperary Spring Water Co. Ltd.), Peter Cullen (Clara Candy Ltd.), Billy Glennon (Vision Information Consulting Ltd.), Paul Higgins (Cahill May Roberts Group), Paul Kavanagh (Donnelly Documentation Services), David Kingston (Irish Life Assurance plc), Liam Lacey (Erin Group), Billy McCann (Craig Gardner/Price Waterhouse), Craig McKinney (Woodchester Investments plc), Martin Naughton (Glen Dimplex), Michael Whelan (Aran Energy).

Playboy of the Western World cast with its executive producer Ann (Walsh).

The smallest and most exclusive Golf Society in the world — 'The Horses of Men' — Phil Flannery, myself, Eddie Dunne and Eamon Condon. Don't be fooled by those boyish smiles — animals of the sward, all.

The Smell of the Lucre,
the Lure of the Muse

Working with Noel Smyth was having a profound effect upon me. I admired Noel's quick brain and his eye for a business opportunity, and he brought me in, in a minor role, on a few major deals.

For instance, I was involved in acquiring designated status for Monarch Properties in the Square in Tallaght. This meant that Tallaght, which had hitherto been a vastly over-populated, under-serviced suburb of Dublin, effectively became a tax-free zone. Suddenly it made good commercial sense for the large department stores and service companies to locate in Tallaght. The designated status was without doubt the economic making of Tallaght. I was also involved in the Aviette deal, in the late eighties, when Noel Smyth, Pascal Taggart and some of their associates bought the ailing H Williams chain of supermarkets and immediately sold on most of the stores for a tidy profit. I was involved in dealing with the Monopolies Commission and with handling the media coverage of the entire transaction.

Also in the late 1980s, Noel invited me to become involved in a film project that was part of a tax arrangement for one of his clients. My function was to look after the everyday running of the movie, keep an eye on the budget and generally act in his and his client's interests. The film was *The Fantasist*, which would star Christopher Cazenove, Cyril Cusack, Timothy Bottoms, a newcomer named Moira Harris and a host of Irish stars.

Cyril Cusack was scheduled to join the unit on the first day. However, his agent called to say that Cyril was double-booked and would be unable to attend for another couple of days. The producer, Mark Forrestal, was under tremendous scheduling pressure and needed to shoot those scenes, with or without Cyril. A decision was taken that Cyril would be dropped from the movie, as he had contravened his contract, and Mick Lally was brought in to play the part. Within a matter of days, Cyril had sued. The newspapers headlined the incident as Cyril suing Mike Murphy of RTE, but in fact I had been unaware of what was happening at the time, and I certainly hadn't made the final decision. Nonetheless, I was now publicly implicated as the 'hatchet man'. Paul Cusack, Cyril's son, who worked with me in RTE, told me that his father's career had suffered irreparable damage because of the incident. However, a settlement was eventually agreed and the movie was completed.

Cyril didn't know how lucky he was. The movie was awful – tasteless, tacky, violent, misogynistic – everything that would make it a successful video rental. And such proved to be the case. There was one weekend, soon after its release as a video, that it was the most successful video rental in the United States. I have no doubt that the cover of the tape contributed in no small measure to its success, as it featured a naked Moira Harris, lying face-down on a bed while a man wielding a knife took photographs of her. I was credited on the movie as Executive Producer. However, I do not include *The Fantasist* among my cinematic achievements!

When cable television came along, I immediately saw its potential. Through Declan, I had met an American named Bob Schmidt, who was involved in the telecommunications business in the US and who asked me to look out for opportunities in Ireland for him. When Cablelink was offered for sale on the open market, I contacted Bob and he came over, bringing with him his associate Curt Bradley. We investigated Cablelink and then put together a consortium to make a bid. Dermot Desmond, who was then head of NCB, was one of the people who joined us. We had made our bid and raised most of the finance when, a few months later, Dermot phoned and invited me to lunch. He told me that he was leaving our consortium to join with Telecom Éireann, who were also bidding and whose Chairman was Dermot's friend, Michael Smurfit.

'Well,' I told Dermot, 'If you're leaving to go over to Telecom Éireann, then I assume they are going to get Cablelink, so it's hardly worth our while staying in the race.'

He said there was no such guarantee, but that he had chosen to go with Michael Smurfit because they were working on other deals as well.

'Why don't you consider buying up the smaller cable systems around Cablelink, while everybody's eye is off the ball?' he suggested.

I thought this was a simply brilliant idea. I went back to Bob and Curt and told them that, if we bought the systems in Malahide, Swords, Naas, Navan and the others that were privately owned by small operators, we could outflank Cablelink totally, while continuing to mount a frontal bid for the company.

Curt and Bob returned to the States and enlisted the professional and financial aid of Tom Keaveney, a highly respected figure in the cable industry who had sold some of his franchises and was looking for new opportunities, preferably in Ireland. The deal was set. Tom wanted to meet me, so he invited me to New York where we had a long question and answer session, went for drinks and then dinner, at the end of which he told me he'd be pleased to go into business with me. He sent me back to set about buying as many systems as I could, whilst he organised the finance in the States. Sean Finlay, a former Cablelink technician, and Tom's son Steve were also involved and Tom himself would come over whenever possible.

We bought the cable systems at Mullingar, Athlone, Greystones, New Ross, Kildare, Naas, Newbridge, Malahide and Swords. Then we went on to Athlone, Sligo, Castlebar and Ballina and, eventually, we applied for and got the MMDS rights to the entire north-west. We spent millions of pounds buying up systems and, during this extraordinary buying spree, I learned a huge amount about business dealing and banking – and even a little about accountancy! I became chairman of CMI Cable (as the new company was called), a title I still hold. Emdee owns a small percentage of CMI, which now has 18 systems and 50,000 subscribers nationwide and is scheduled to sign up many more.

In February 1989, I was nominated *Irish Press* Business Person of the Month and was one of twelve nominees as Business Person of the Year. We were expanding Emdee now, as the company became more successful, and, although Larry and I were doing our best on the production and general administration side, we felt we needed more expertise.

I phoned Seamus O'Neill, who, when he was advertising manager with the *Irish Times*, had been headhunted by Oliver Barry for Century Radio. Century had since collapsed and Seamus had joined Vincent Browne at the *Sunday Tribune*. When we met in the Berkeley Court, I outlined the plans Larry and I had for Emdee's expansion, the nature of our needs and the benefits that would be his should he care to join us. A few days later, Seamus called to say that he would be delighted to join us and that he was looking forward to the challenge. As I write, he is still managing director of Emdee Productions, having survived a few lean years in the independent film sector.

In 1990, Larry and I decided to move office, as Emdee was expanding rapidly. This time we took a major gamble and bought a building of twelve and a half thousand square feet in Sheriff Street, borrowing almost one hundred per cent of the finance. Many people thought we were mad moving into an area that had the reputation of being 'bandit country', but we were delighted to get such a large building and, besides, I felt sure the area would improve in time.

We were the first new business in the area in many years, so Larry and I visited the church in Sheriff Street where I spoke to the local people, from the altar, about our plans. We told them that we intended to create jobs in the area and that we hoped that we would all enjoy a mutually beneficial and pleasant relationship.

When the building had been refurbished, Emdee moved in, followed by CMI, then a small advertising agency, and a marketing and design company, Target Marketing. Others soon followed. When the building was full, we were able, as we had promised, to offer jobs to the locals. This was not without incident, however, and at times some tough talking was necessary. There were a few local 'hard men' who had to be dealt with and, on some occasions, we resorted to unorthodox methods. I recall spotting two of 'the boys' robbing the local bookie's, while the bookie himself was out for a sandwich. I challenged the two culprits in the street a couple of days later, telling them it was a 'dreadful thing about the way the poor bookie was robbed' and that it was a 'couple of people he trusted' who had done it. There was a sullen silence and then one of them asked me what was I talking about. So I explained that, if anything happened to our building, I would feel obliged to report what had happened at the bookie's to the police. I asked them if we understood each other and they responded in the affirmative. So we had no further trouble from that quarter!

'Sniffy' Duggan was a bit of a celebrity in the area. Whenever Sniffy was 'on holiday' from Mountjoy Prison, we knew we had to keep a close eye on the cars. Sniffy was forever in trouble with the law, but the guards were reputed to be somewhat apprehensive about him ever since he let it to be known that he had contracted the Aids virus and would bite if arrested! Sniffy is possessed of a long, humourless, pock-marked face, with shifty eyes. He favours flashy anoraks and walks in a brisk, business-like manner, ever on the alert for a bit of action. One particular morning, Sniffy was caught breaking into one of the CMI vans. Three of the CMI lads cornered him, appealing to his better nature and telling him that they were only trying to do their jobs. Sniffy immediately looked indignant and, pointing to himself, shouted, 'I'm only doing my job, too, you know.' Further discussion was pointless and there the matter ended, but I don't believe Sniffy has created any bother for us since.

There was, needless to say, some pilfering from cars but, whenever something was taken, we were able to get it back through our various 'contacts' in the Sheriff Street flats. I recall one occasion when my golf clubs had been stolen from the boot of the car, outside my house in Foxrock. The insurance inspector was due at my office to question me about the matter and was well over half an hour late. When he eventually arrived, looking extremely flushed, he explained what had happened. He had been driving down Sheriff Street when he saw a child lying motionless in the road. Naturally, he stopped the car and got out, but, as he did so, the child got up and ran away. While he was distracted, another couple of kids opened the boot of his car and ran away with – yes, you've guessed it – his golf clubs! A short while later, one of them came back from the flats, wearing a golf cap which looked very familiar, and asked him if he would like his clubs back.

'If you give us a hundred quid, you can have them,' they said. He refused. Although angry and shaken, he did see the humour of the situation, and was gracious enough not to ask me any questions at all about *my* claim. He asked me if there was any chance of getting the clubs back, and within a day or so he had them!

In 1991, Norma Smurfit invited Eileen and me to attend the Oscars in Hollywood – this was a dream come true for Eileen. We travelled in the Smurfit jet with our friends Gay and Irene Moloney and Ken and Nuala Wall, as well as Norma, and arrived at the theatre in the middle of the afternoon, where the mandatory Oscar crowd was waiting to greet their favourite stars. We, naturally, were completely overlooked, as the fans cast around for famous faces. As we were about to enter the theatre, I heard a voice call from the crowd, 'Hey, Mick, what are you doing here?'

I turned around, and discovered it was Tom Myler of the *Evening Herald*, who was standing at the crash barrier, celebrity-spotting. Tom was very impressed, I can tell you, to see us all 'dolled up' to attend the ceremonies.

And a fascinating experience it was, too. Daniel Day Lewis and Brenda Fricker were to be the eventual recipients of the little gold statuettes, but, immediately before the show, the organisers couldn't find Daniel Day Lewis. They had only seen him on screen as Christy Brown in a wheelchair, and so the ushers were asking people if they had seen a guy in a wheelchair, as they had a seat reserved for him, as well as a ramp, but couldn't find him. We were seated near the back of the theatre and I caught a glimpse of Daniel standing shyly behind a pillar, wearing a long evening coat and with his hair shoulder-length for his part in *The Last of the Mohicans*. In terms of Christy Brown, he is unrecognisable and, being the shy and reserved person he is, was not going to make himself known. It was not until the curtain was about to go up that somebody recognised him and frogmarched him to his seat.

During the course of the ceremony, which was about three hours long, people in the audience kept leaving their seats, to go for a drink or to the toilets. Outside each of the theatre doors was a queue of very well-dressed actors and actresses. These were the 'seaters'. As soon as anyone stepped out to go to the toilet or for a drink, a seater – male if it was the man who stepped out, female if it was the woman – immediately took their place, so that at no stage was there a vacant seat in the auditorium. These people were paid an appearance fee for the occasion.

During the show I went downstairs to the gents and, when I was returning, saw Daniel Day Lewis in the bar on his own. I had met Daniel some months previously in Dublin and he remembered the occasion and asked me to join him for a drink. He was quite agitated. He said he didn't know why he had come and that he had no chance whatsoever of winning an Oscar. However, we agreed that, if by any chance he did, we would meet for a drink after the show in exactly the same place. When he won, he sought me out and said, 'Come on, let's have that drink.' Which is exactly what we did – in the appointed place. Brenda Fricker was overjoyed with her award and was only too happy to have her photo taken with all and sundry, clutching her Oscar. Afterwards we went to Spago's, then to Jimmy Murphy's restaurant, and from there to some private parties, in true Hollywood fashion.

In the foyer of the theatre, before the Oscar ceremony, I bumped into an old golfing partner of mine, the movie actor Jack Lemmon. About two years previously, Jack and I had been invited to play in the John A Mulcahy Classic in Waterville, County Kerry. Jack Mulcahy, now sadly gone, was one of the gentlest and finest men I have ever met. I knew him well over a number of years and was very sad that he ultimately lost control of the golf course he had created and of Ashford and Dromoland Castles. Anyway, Jack Lemmon and I were drawn in the same fourball, which meant that we would play golf together for the four days of the tournament. When we teed off on the first day, there was a crowd of about five hundred watching, all wanting to see Jack, who proved to be a delightful, outgoing character. However, we had noticed that he had a little white plastic cup and that he kept kneeling down at his golf bag and fiddling around. What we didn't know until later was that he had a bottle of vodka in his bag and was 'topping up' as we went round the course. On the second hole, our challenge fell apart when Jack's drive went into the rough. He took a three-wood from his bag. There were murmurs from the crowd. They knew that he had taken out the wrong club, that he would need to play a wedge or a nine-iron to get out of that 'lie'. Jack strolled over to the ball, reached down and ripped up a few handfuls of grass to give himself a better lie. The crowd and his fellow team members groaned; he had broken almost every rule in the book in improving his lie in that way. We were thereby disqualified from the tournament. Fortunately, we went on to play so badly as to be out of the running anyway, so we did not tell Jack that we had already been automatically disqualified.

For the next two days, the two Irish players, myself and Irish international Arthur Pierse, and Jack and an American professional, had tremendous fun playing against each other as a Ryder Cup; Ireland versus the United States in this case.

I have made many friends through golf and have the privilege of being a member of one of the smallest and most distinguished golfing societies in the world, known quaintly as the 'Horses of Men'. The group consists of just four members – Phil Flannery, Eamon Condon, Eddie Dunne and myself – friends of long standing, from quite disparate backgrounds. Eamon, witty, stocky and good-humoured, is well known in banking circles as the manager of the College Green branch of the Bank of Ireland, and is a ferocious competitor on the golf course. Phil Flannery, a self-made entrepreneur who is now retired and travels the world enjoying the fruits of his labour may not be the best golfer of the four but, even though older than the rest of us, is the most hardy – and best able for long hours and short drinks. Quiet-spoken, droll Eddie Dunne, formerly an international golfer and currently selector for Connaught, was recently appointed as golfing director for the new and exclusive Druid's Glen Golf Club in County Wicklow. We four have played golf in Spain and all over Ireland, and have greatly enjoyed each other's company through the years.

Then there is Noel O'Neill, another friend of long standing, who is very well known and liked in golfing circles. He walks with a severe limp as a result of polio and, like myself, he is a member of Royal Dublin Golf Club. Noel is the central character in a story that almost every golfer in Ireland knows. Christy O'Connor was entertaining Lionel Platts and Hedley Muscroft, two of the great golfers of their time, at the Royal Dublin, and Christy's partner had not turned up. Christy, knowing that Noel had a handicap of seventeen, invited him to play, and Noel was thrilled to accept. A very significant amount of money was placed on the outcome of the game – all three of the professionals were big gamblers – but Noel was spared the financial side, being an amateur. Noel played superbly, and Christy and Noel duly won the match. When they had finished the eighteenth, Noel limped off with the others, and Hedley Muscroft called after him.

'Noel,' he said, 'You can stop your limping now, you've won the money.' He was mortified when he found out later that the limp was not an act. Noel, however, thought it was utterly hilarious.

When Noel was captain of Royal Dublin, he had to make a speech at the televised final of the Carroll's Irish Open. He was very nervous about appearing in front of so many people, and about speaking to a television audience. He asked me to help with his speech, which I did, suggesting also that he include a quote or two from Oscar Wilde. Noel delivered himself of these Wildean quotes, crediting the ubiquitous Oscar, of course, and he hasn't lived it down since. Every time he misses a putt, his opponent will invariably ask what Oscar would have said in the same circumstances. I am sure he wishes he had asked Niall Tóibín – another member – for advice, instead of me.

Niall is a great friend of ours, but there are those in Royal Dublin who don't have the necessary stamina to weather a Tóibín outburst on the golf course. He can be awesome, and he's not a bad golfer sometimes, either! I recall the round of golf I played with Niall the day that the Committee was to consider his application for full membership. Four of us played, including Noel O'Neill and another old friend of ours, Bill O'Herlihy of TV sports fame. Bill had never previously played with Niall and, even before the game was over, he had decided that he would never play with him again! Niall has a disconcerting habit of roaring at his partner if they fluff a shot.

Anyway, playing the eighteenth hole, which doglegs around the garden and finishes up directly under the big bay window of the Members' Bar, Niall was in a spot of bother. Bill had hit his ball out of bounds and was looking suitably penitent, and both Noel and I were on the green in three. Niall's ball was just short of the bunker and it was essential that he get it on the green if they were to have a chance of a win. He gritted his teeth, lined up the shot, and then struck. The ball went straight into the bunker! The bay window was full of spectators, including members of the Committee, who were about to go into session to decide who should have the honour of joining the club. Just as Noel shouted, 'Niall, don't!' Niall threw his club with utter ferocity at the ball and proceeded to berate the ball, in very colourful language, for going into the bunker. That evening, Noel had to plead the case for Niall's inclusion as a member, and must have done so with Wildean distinction because Niall was accepted and has been a full member now for many years.

Those first business years were a stimulating and heady period in my life. I devoured the business pages of newspapers and magazines. I knew the value of every company on the Dublin stock exchange, the daily currency rates, and the names of the chief executives and chairmen of the top five hundred companies in Ireland. I found that I had an eye for an opportunity and enjoyed initiating a project, but that, once it was up and running, boredom would soon set in.

In 1988, Brian Mac Aonghasa, who was Controller of Radio in RTE, discussed with producer Colin Morrison the possibility of creating a new arts programme. Knowing of my interest in the visual arts, cinema, theatre and books, they invited me to be the presenter. *The Arts Show* was a programme which was ideally suited to my interests and background.

Despite some initial hostility to my presenting the programme (there were those who considered me to be an intellectual lightweight) I have become recognised as someone who can make the arts more accessible to the general public. In the late seventies and early eighties, when I first became actively involved in the arts, I came to realise that there was an élite group in Dublin who monopolised the visual arts. They were the arbiters of taste; they determined which artists would be selected for major exhibitions, who would be nominated to the Arts Council, and so on. *The Arts Show* gave me an opportunity to be more democratic, and to bring the arts to a wider audience.

I often have heated debates with the curators and directors of galleries about the arcane and exclusive language they use in their catalogue entries and articles about the visual arts. I have often found these almost incomprehensible and I work on the basis that, if I find them difficult to understand, then so do a lot of other people. While acknowledging that there are undoubtedly a range of terms which are specific to art appreciation, I do not approve of a policy of excluding the vast majority of enthusiasts, potential enthusiasts, and even sometimes arts practitioners themselves.

I recall one occasion when I was asked to open an exhibition of Patrick Graham's work. Graham is one of the best and most successful artists of his time. Having read the introductory essay to his catalogue, written by the director of the gallery in which the launch was to take place, I asked the director to explain some of the terms he had used. I have been a fan of Paddy's for many years and I took issue with some of the director's interpretations of his work. He took me over to one of the larger paintings and explained that, in Paddy's work, he, the director, could see contemporary Ireland, that there were references to child molestation, the role of the church, even the beef tribunal and angel dust. I called Patrick Graham over to join us and asked him if he had intended to include any of these themes in his work.

'Certainly not,' said Paddy, looking totally mystified. 'Not intentionally anyway.'

I felt I had made a point, but the director was having none of it, insisting that he would stand over his interpretation. This once again demonstrated quite clearly for me that many of the more influential people in the art world are merely writing and interpreting for each other.

My workload for *The Arts Show* is quite heavy. Usually, I have to read two or three books each weekend, and I like to attend the movies, plays and exhibitions we are going to review in order to form my own opinion. Very occasionally, if I attend a play which is particularly bad, I will wait until the interval and do what Michael Colgan of the Gate

Theatre refers to as 'Murphy's runner'. I leave as discreetly as possible! I used to feel guilty about this, but I have long since rationalised it on the basis that life is too short to be wasted on something that is neither enjoyable nor fulfilling.

Despite having resolved, a number of years previously, not to return to daytime radio, as I had no interest in presenting a chat show or playing records, Kevin Healy, the Director of Radio, persuaded me to move with *The Arts Show* into its current daytime slot.

The Arts Show ran for seven years on Tuesday, Wednesday and Thursday at 7 o'clock. In January of this year, it was moved to Monday, Tuesday and Wednesday afternoons, with a 'highlights' programme on Thursday evenings. The move didn't please everyone, particularly those of the business community who enjoyed listening to the programme as they drove home from work, and many in the artistic community also felt strongly that the time was unsuitable.

Over the years, a number of producers and researchers have worked with me on the programme, talented people like Colin Morrison, Seamus Hosey, Doireann Ní Bhriain, Paddy Glacken, Micheál Holmes and others, each of them contributing their own particular expertise. I feel, however, that our current staff of Ann Walsh, Yetti Redmond, Bernadette Comerford, Eamonn Sweeney and Catriona O'Connell is perhaps the strongest, in terms of a team, we have ever had.

I have been very fortunate, through my involvement in the arts, to make the acquaintance of, and in many cases become friends with, such distinguished people as the late Michael Scott, Gordon Lambert, Tony and Jane O'Malley, Pat and Antoinette Murphy, Sean and Rosemarie Mulcahy, Anthony Cronin, Seamus and Marie Heaney, Noel Sheridan, Ciaran MacGonigal, Declan McGonagle, and many more. I also feel privileged to have known the likes of Benedict Kiely, Ciarán Mac Mathúna, Donal Foley, Sean J White, Sean MacReamonn, John Ryan and many more of the so-called 'Celtic intellectuals'. We have a unique heritage and it is right and proper that we appreciate our artists and writers while they are still alive.

I have spoken long and often about my attitude to the arts. I don't like the capital 'A' that regularly appears at the beginning of the word. Ask people whether they are interested in the arts and many will reply 'No'. Ask them if they go to movies, watch TV, read books, listen to music, and they are likely to answer 'Yes'. These *are* the arts. Add in paintings, poetry, photography, theatre and so on and you have a complete portfolio. I want people to lose their inhibitions about going to commercial or State art galleries, to read the poems of John Montague, Michael Hartnett, Seamus Heaney, Paul Durcan, Eavan Boland and see what feelings or reactions they invoke, to go to movies that may not be mainstream Hollywood, and to simply open themselves to a world of wonder and revelation that need not cost any more money than they would normally spend. I would also like them to listen, when possible, to *The Arts Show*, where there is always something new, or provocative, or different, or even just relevant. For me, *The Arts Show* has been like a privileged and intensive third-level education, and I would like others to share in whatever opportunities it may present.

In 1989, *Winning Streak* came along. It was the brainchild of David Blake Knox and Kevin Linehan, in conjunction with Ray Bates of the National Lottery. I was delighted when I was approached to present the programme, and felt confident that it would be a huge success. Initially, Ray and RTE were reluctant to allow the participants to be interviewed, but I relished the challenge of making 'people off the street' feel comfortable on television. I felt that I would be able to handle most situations and that viewers would enjoy relating to the various participants. I suggested a trial period of three programmes where participants were interviewed, but, if this proved unsuccessful, we would revert to the original concept of announcing the names of the players, showing a shot of them and getting on with the game. It soon became apparent that the informal 'interviews' were very popular and that viewers got a kick out of people describing their own lives, often with a good deal of humour. The programme was an instant hit and, even now, seven years later, is seldom out of the top five in the TAM ratings.

I am often asked if there is a conflict for me between presenting two such different programmes as *The Arts Show* and *Winning Streak*. However, both reflect different facets of my own personality and I derive great satisfaction from each of them. When presenting *Winning Streak*, I aim to make the players as relaxed as possible, as this is a big day in their lives. I use the very Irish ploy of 'slagging' and teasing and this is usually successful in putting them at their ease. Prior to going on air, I do a warm-up with the audience and, on a given cue from me, the director rolls the clock and we are on the air without any tension building up between the warm-up and the beginning of the programme. I try to make it all as seamless as possible.

There have, of course, been moments I would like to forget. The worst was when we featured a gentleman who had very prominent teeth. As it happened, he was the one who qualified to 'spin the wheel', and, as we walked towards the wheel, I heard a voice saying 'Spin it with your teeth'. It was with abject horror that I realised the voice belonged to me!

Winning Streak is transmitted on Saturdays, which means that I am unable to take a weekend off for three-quarters of the year, but I still enjoy it enormously and regard it as an important part of my professional life. Over the years, Ray Bates and myself, who share a mutual interest in the arts, wine and food, have formed a strong friendship, and we have a standing arrangement to treat each other to a good meal out every other month.

An End and a Beginning

I first met Ann Walsh in 1988. I had been presenting *The Arts Show* for a matter of months when Ann, who was a trainee producer, joined the team for a short period on a placement. I was immediately attracted to her. She was lovely – of medium height, with strong classical features, striking blue eyes, light brown hair and a dazzling smile. I think what struck me most about her was her innate quality of stillness. There was nothing fidgety or nervous about her, nothing coy. She would quietly observe everything that was going on around her and, when making eye contact, she would look at you quite candidly, without any hint of flirtation.

One night, as I was leaving RTE to go to a play in the Project, I met Ann who was also on her way out. I asked her, if she was doing nothing else, would she like to come with me, and she agreed. Eileen normally accompanied me to plays, but she had been unable to make it on this particular evening. I can't remember the name of the play but it was pretty abysmal, and, at the interval, I suggested to Ann that we leave and maybe go for a bite to eat. She was quite shocked at the notion of leaving before the end, but she was also intrigued. We slipped out and went to a nearby restaurant.

Over dinner, Ann told me her story. At twenty she had married a lecturer in Trinity and had two boys, then aged fourteen and eight. The marriage was not a success. She had left her husband and now lived on her own with the children. I told her about myself, that I was in a good marriage with Eileen, that I worked from dawn to dusk, that I loved my children and that I led a full and interesting life. We left the restaurant, I drove her back to her car, we said goodnight and that was that. While I was attracted to her, I had no intention of suggesting any further contact. Later, I found out that Ann had also felt an attraction, but we were both aware of the risks involved in pursuing further intimacy.

Ann had taken a year's leave of absence from her teaching job at Wesley College to try her hand at research and production in RTE. She worked for a while in television and then qualified for the radio producers' course. In time, she was appointed to *The Gay Byrne Show* as a producer.

Over the next few years, we met casually in RTE, exchanged a few words, and went our separate ways. She had by then formed a relationship with somebody else and was living with him. Then, a few years ago, we met by accident in Belfast where I was working on a possible cable TV deal. We went out to dinner together and commenced a clandestine relationship.

Why did I do it? I had a good marriage with Eileen and a happy home life. I knew that someone with as public a profile as myself ran a grave risk of being found out and I knew the consequences would be unthinkable; Eileen would be so hurt she would be unable to forgive me.

One of my reasons for writing this memoir is to explore the possible causes of the breakdown of my marriage. As I write, I can see that all along there were tell-tale signs. My life was led 'on the hoof', so to speak. Eileen's mother had told her that I was a 'runner', as she called it, and that I would never stay with her. My mother, I found out years later, had also forecast that the marriage would not last. Certainly, if blame is to be apportioned, then I willingly shoulder most of it. I was a workaholic, obsessed with living my life to the full and in need of constant stimulation.

Eileen was always far calmer than me, more contained, more contented. She was happy to live a glamorous life through me, and she also had four lovely children of whom she thought the world. Eileen's mother had died while I was in Australia, and so now both her parents were dead. She had no brothers or sisters and she was not close to any of her relations. With the death of Gran, and as the children began to move away from home, Eileen became more reliant on me for company.

However, over the years our interests had diverged, and, although we still got on extremely well together, I know that I had become quite selfish with my time. I needed time to read, to visit galleries, to watch movies, and I didn't always feel a need for Eileen to accompany me. I frequently became irritated, accusing her of trying to turn my work into a social occasion, and this became a bone of contention between us. I have no excuse, however, for starting my relationship with Ann. It happened. And it continued, sporadically, over a few years. At no stage did I tell Ann that I was unhappy in my marriage and neither did she ask me to leave, even though her relationship at that time was failing.

In late 1994, I went with Ann for a weekend in Paris, and shortly after Eileen found out. There was an appalling scene. Eileen was unspeakably shocked and wounded, and she ordered me out of the house. I moved into the Conrad Hotel, where my friend Michael Governey was extremely kind to me, although he had no real idea of what was going on. I told Ann I needed time to think. I hardly left my room for three days. Eileen contacted me to say she would take me back if I wanted to come back. I returned to the house and, in an emotional meeting with Eileen and my children, told them that I wanted to come home.

By now, Ann's relationship had broken up and she had bought her own house in Ballinteer and was working as a producer on *The Arts Show*. We tried to keep everything on a professional footing, avoiding each other as far as possible both inside and outside of the office. It was difficult. In the summer, I went to the United States for a month on my own to mull things over; I was feeling very depressed. When I returned, Eileen was waiting for me at Shannon Airport and we went on to spend a week in a holiday cottage near Ballyvaughan in County Clare. The interlude wasn't a success in terms of reviving our marriage. We got back to Dublin and, although I didn't tell Eileen, I began to see Ann again. Within a few weeks, Eileen had discovered my deception.

We tried to sort things out, and even had relationship counselling, but we knew we had to come to terms with reality. We endured agonies of depression and had endless and savage rows. Then Eileen gave me an ultimatum. I was to stop seeing Ann and have her transferred from *The Arts Show*, or else the marriage was over. I told her I wasn't prepared to do that. We limped along for another few weeks and then, just before Christmas, after a particularly vicious row, I packed and left. I moved into an apartment in Blackrock and, although I have visited my family home on a regular basis since, I have never stayed overnight.

The *Sunday Independent* knew of my relationship with Ann, through their contacts in RTE. Terry Keane phoned me and said that, whether I liked it or not, they were going to run the story the following Sunday. I spoke with Eileen, who said it was time I stopped 'dithering about' and that we should acknowledge the fact that the marriage was over. She suggested we make a joint statement to that effect.

Terry Keane and Aengus Fanning, the editor of the *Sunday Independent*, agreed to my conditions that I would have total editorial control over the story. On the Friday, I was working with Ann in Callan, County Kilkenny, where I was interviewing the painters Tony and Jane O'Malley for an *Arts Show* special. There was a constant stream of phone calls between myself and Eileen and the newspaper. Eventually, the wording of the announcement was agreed. The *Sunday Independent* printed their exclusive.

Even now, I can hardly bear to think of the hurt and shock the whole episode caused our children. Elaine and Carol had known for some time that a break-up was likely and both responded in a very mature and even-handed way. Deirdre and Mark, on the other hand, were so devastated that for a while they could hardly bear to speak to me. Our friends, likewise, were quite traumatised by the break-up; we had always appeared to be the ideal couple. In fact, afterwards, we learned that many of them found themselves questioning their own marriages.

Eileen was shocked at the revelation that the affair had been going on for so long and understandably resentful of my having put herself and the children through such an unthinkable public and private humiliation. Though hurt and angry, she maintained her dignity throughout. Ann was predictably seen by the newspapers as the 'scarlet woman' and, but for the support of her family and friends, might have found it impossible to cope. I was in a turmoil of guilt and despair. I couldn't sleep and it was difficult to concentrate at work. I continued to live in my little apartment in Blackrock.

I kept in touch with the children, trying hard to be honest with them and impressing on them that, whatever they thought about what I had done, I needed them in my life.

Gradually, the shock and hurt has subsided. Public reaction wasn't as harsh as I had feared. Eileen and I re-established more regular contact and the children began to lose their anger and resentment. I am now in touch almost daily with all my children and we see each other as often as we can. Eileen and I reached an amicable financial settlement and I eventually moved in to Ann's house and also bought a small apartment in the city centre.

Who can tell what the future will hold? Ann and I are extremely happy together. We share common interests and spend most of our free time together. We have a loving, companionable relationship. Eileen has sold the family home and has moved with Elaine and Mark into a smaller house in south County Dublin, while Carol and Deirdre live in apartments in Dublin. We have all come through a very dark and difficult couple of years.

Montrose, by any other Name. . .

As I write, John McColgan, Moya Doherty and another very good friend of mine, Brian Molloy, are part of a consortium which has been granted the new National Radio Licence. I am very pleased for them. If anybody can make a success of the venture, it's this threesome and their backers. RTE just might need to look to its laurels. I know that senior and middle management in radio are trying to adjust to the realities of competition in the home market, and there may be a good deal of adjusting to be done. There is an insularity about RTE that urgently needs to be addressed. As chief executive of Emdee Productions, I was in the vanguard of the independent film sector for many years, where I witnessed its disgraceful treatment by middle management in television at RTE. We were forced to grovel, to beg, and ultimately to threaten, to get a single crumb from that table. I have seen a character as tough as my friend and partner, Larry Masterson, almost reduced to tears of anger and frustration at the indignities heaped upon him. It is not my wish to bite the hand that feeds me, but I have made these comments quite forcefully within the organisation. RTE needs to adopt a more respectful and open approach if it is going to survive the challenges and changes in store.

And change is inevitable, both on television and on radio. Gay Byrne, who is almost irreplaceable, is already signalling that he is likely to move on in the near future. This will be the catalyst for change. We, his fellow broadcasters, regard Gay as the greatest professional of them all. He is an interviewer *par excellence*. He gives his undivided attention to his subject, looking them directly in the eye, has memorised his research and, if he looks at his notes, it's in an entirely natural way, almost as part of the conversation. He can gauge public taste and whims and is not afraid to plough his own furrow.

There will, quite simply, *never* be another Gay Byrne. With the fragmentation of the choices on offer nowadays, no one person in the future will ever monopolise or dominate the airwaves as he has done. The fact that Gay's influence has been almost entirely positive in terms of the example he has set, the issues he has tackled and the sheer downright honesty of his personality is something of which he can be truly proud.

Is Gay Byrne the great liberal that people say he is? I don't believe so. In many ways, Gay is the ultimate conservative and his liberal tendencies have simply reflected the general public's need for change. On a personal level, I like Gay tremendously – we are friends. He is a decent and honourable man who will help those in difficulties. I will miss him greatly if and when he retires – if I am still around to see the day!

What about the rest of us? How do we compare to Gay? *Do* we compare? Supposing RTE were to retain *The Late Late Show* in a post-GB era, who would be chosen as host? (And why am I even bothering to indulge in this whimsical pastime of musical microphones?)

Before embarking on some frivolous and harmless musings about these mythical succession stakes, let me try to do a 'warts and all' assessment of my own position as a broadcaster. Firstly, I have not the slightest interest in presenting a chat-type show on television. I do not wish to be the instrument whereby those who have suffered are invited to suffer a little more, and publicly this time, with a few tears if possible, for the delectation of the greater Irish viewer. Besides, I would probably find some of the stories too emotional to handle without being visibly affected myself.

I irritate myself by saying 'Yeah' when my interviewee is speaking, I sometimes ask overly-long questions, and overall I probably haven't committed myself fully to my chosen profession. I think I am slightly embarrassed by the facile way that fame and admiration come the way of even untalented TV 'personalities'. (By the way, I do not include myself in the latter category. Dammit, modesty is one thing, pride is another!)

But, back to the whimsy. Will there be a Gay Byrne Mark Two?

Pat Kenny? I'm not sure. Although he is an extremely intelligent man, with an encyclopaedic grasp of facts and figures, Pat often doesn't elicit information or emotion with the same shrewdness as Gay. He is all too obviously thinking of the next question, who's standing where, technical matters, and so on. Gay does all those things, but it is not so apparent. I don't mean to denigrate Pat's professionalism in any way, in fact I admire him a great deal, but I think his desire for perfection sometimes blinds him to his own limitations.

How about Gerry Ryan? Well, Gerry is superb on radio, fast, free-wheeling, provocative, utterly at ease. Television? I don't know. He's had a succession of pretty disastrous TV shows and even his most recent one languished at the rear end of the ratings. I don't think it's a coincidence that all the really successful Irish TV personalities – Byrne, Frank Hall, Pat Kenny, myself – had the instincts and often the title of 'Producer'. It's a canniness, an ability to forecast the reaction to an item you're about to do, a refusal to get carried away with the euphoria of some 'priceless' in-joke, the nerve to say 'No, that won't work'. Some little discernment. Will Gerry develop it? I hope so. He's too good to miss out on the TV success that is his due.

Marian Finucane? A once-off. Wonderful on radio, true to herself with all her natural little foibles of 'em'-ing, coughing, constant admonitions of 'Ah, hold on there a minute' adding to rather than detracting from her programmes. She has found her *métier* in *Liveline* and long may it continue. TV? Marian does very nicely thank you on

Crimeline (what's with all these '-lines'?) and is very happy to meander quietly along in her chosen niche.

There are many other fine broadcasters in RTE: Derek Davis, Brendan Balfe, Myles Dungan, Miriam O'Callaghan, Ronan Collins, Brian Farrell, Ian Dempsey, Larry Gogan, John Bowman, Dave Fanning, John Creedon, Treasa Davison, Ruth Buchanan and Joe Duffy, not to mention the news and sports teams. But it is invidious to even start mentioning names and I don't wish to in any way diminish those I may have inadvertently omitted.

In summary, however, despite the extraordinarily high standard of broadcasting of which RTE can boast, old Gaybo remains the standard by which all shall be judged. And there's simply no one to touch him. It could be said that RTE should have invested time and money in selecting and nurturing a successor, but I would argue that the man is unique, and reiterate that we shall not see his like again.

As regards my own broadcasting future, who knows? Many years ago, Tom McGrath advised me to follow a different path to Gay's, not to try to emulate him, not to stand in for him when he goes on holiday, to create my own individualistic broadcasting persona. I still want to do more TV along the lines of *Murphy's America* and *Murphy's Australia*, but for the present *The Arts Show*, *Winning Streak* and the *Proms* suit me just fine.

As I have mentioned, this will be a time of natural fragmentation of the market. RTE, despite its financial limitations, is one of the best broadcasting organisations in the world. While I am sometimes critical of management practices, I genuinely feel that the station's output is never less than top class and I am extremely proud to have been associated with RTE through these ground-breaking years. It is not for me to judge the merits of my own contribution, but I would like to think that, along with my fellow presenters and producers, I have played a small part in the remarkable and historical changes that have taken place in Irish society during the past thirty years.

Epilogue

I'm 54 years of age as I write this. Hopefully, it's too premature to have been my autobiography. Like the song says, there are many more places to see and things to do before I take my regretful leave of this life.

I have written this memoir for two reasons. Firstly, I had reached a cathartic moment in my own life and I needed to know some of the reasons for its advent. Why was I permitting all I held dear and everything for which I had worked so hard to come crashing down around me? And secondly, my career as a broadcaster coincided with both the birth and the halcyon years of RTE television and revolutionary changes in radio. With the current volatility of the world of electronic media, the monopoly we enjoyed in RTE is well and truly over, and it seems timely to record my memories of that singular thirty-year period.

I live life at a hundred miles an hour. I read voraciously, love theatre and films, derive immense pleasure from paintings, sculpture and all aspects of the visual arts, will watch nature films and sport on TV, play golf, love travel and adventure, and enjoy eating out and good wines.

I don't like bureaucracy, grey people, unkindness, DIY or gardening. I have little interest in cars, clothes, image or impressing others. I enjoy anecdotes more than jokes and don't feel any great desire to meet 'new' people. I try to avoid first nights, dinner parties and dress dances. I don't want my name in the papers, and the novelty of being recognised wore off about twenty-five years ago. My life with Ann is low-key, exclusive, interesting, loving and, most of all, fulfilling.

I have known sadness, fear and joy. I respect courage. I have loved and been loved by two exceptional women, and I wish I could express better the love I feel for my children.

Is there something terrible looming? I hope not. But, as I have often said to my family, I have led three or four lives in one and know how lucky I am to have been able to do so. Whatever happens, I have little cause for complaint. Is there a next life? I hope so. But even if there is, it risks being pretty boring after this one.

Index

Numbers in italics refer to illustrations and captions.
Mc is treated as Mac, also O' and Ó are treated as if the same.

253